The
Handbook
of Foreign
Student
Advising

The Handbook of Foreign Student Advising

Gary Althen

Intercultural Press, Inc.

Library of Congress Catalogue Card No. 83-082532
ISBN 0-933662-53-X

Printed in the United States of America

Acknowledgments

Many people contributed in one way or another to the production of this book. David Hoopes, Josef Mestenhauser, Richard Brislin, and Roberto Clemente provided inspiration. Several colleagues were generous enough to read the manuscript and offer their suggestions and observations. They include Francis Musa Boakari, Barbara Clark, Catherine Dugan, Janeen Felsing, Virginia Gross, Barbara Halpin, Albert Hood, Martin Limbird, Josef Mestenhauser, Dennis Peterson, Ahmad Reza Riahinejad, Leslie Rowe, Eugene Smith, Karen Towers, and C. Wayne Young. I am deeply grateful to all these helpful individuals.

My wife, Sandy, also read the manuscript and helped make it clearer and more appropriately worded.

Mary Anders unselfishly guided me through the word processing aspects of writing and revision. Peggy Pusch reviewed the manuscript and saw it through production.

My debt to David Hoopes goes back many years, to the time when I was a novice in the foreign student field and he was my supervisor and mentor. He has continued to offer support, encouragement, and a worthy example. This book has benefitted extensively from his sensitivities as an editor.

It should be emphasized that not all of the people who reviewed the manuscript of this *Handbook* agree with everything it says. Some of their suggestions were incorporated into the final version, and others were not. Errors or misjudgments that may be found in these pages are my own.

Gary Althen
Iowa City, Iowa
June, 1983

Contents

Introduction

Foreign student advising is "the most interesting job on the campus," I often tell people. What makes it interesting is the variety of people one meets and the diversity of tasks the job entails. Foreign student advisers (FSA's) may talk in a single day with students from Brazil, Malaysia, Egypt, and several other countries. At larger educational institutions, they might also see visiting scholars from Japan, the United Kingdom, and elsewhere. In addition, FSA's deal with U.S. students, faculty, and staff throughout their institutions. And they work with community volunteers, personnel from U.S. and foreign governmental agencies, and various non-profit educational organizations.

FSA's function as counselors, advisers, administrators, writers, speakers, paralegals, ombudsmen, mediators, and teachers. They may fill all these roles in the course of a given day, switching from one to another at a moment's notice. This variety of functions, clients, and contacts makes it very difficult for a foreign student adviser to become bored.

The case study recounted in Appendix A, "Do You Trust Your Foreign Student?", reflects the complexity of the demands FSA's can face. This case study exemplifies a number of aspects of foreign student advising, and will be referred to again later in the *Handbook*.

Unlike true "professionals," FSA's do not have to complete any specific educational program to obtain their positions. They do not need to pass an examination or obtain a license to practice; they have no professional association that enforces an agreed-upon set of standards. They take no oath of office. In the absence of procedures or regulations that would promote some uniformity in their outlooks and practices, foreign student advisers are left to develop their own notions of what they should be doing and how they should be doing it. In the process of developing those notions, FSA's face countless ethical and practical quandaries.

This *Handbook* is intended to help FSA's as they face those quandaries. It is based on ten years of experience as an FSA at a large public university, consulting at other types of institutions, reading in different disciplines, talking with colleagues, carrying out assorted responsibilities for the National Association for Foreign Student Affairs, writing articles, and reflecting on what I was doing.

As a handbook, this publication emphasizes practical matters. But it includes theoretical material as well. In some ways, the theory is of great practical value. It provides impetus and direction. It gives a context to day-to-day situations. Having a theoretical framework into which to place immediate problems gives an FSA perspective and guidance.

The earlier chapters of the *Handbook* are the more theoretical ones. Chapter One discusses the practical and the conceptual setting in which foreign student advisers work. Chapter Two concerns the nature of the foreign student adviser's position. Chapter Three discusses the personal characteristics of successful FSA's and Chapter Four examines some general attitudes and ideas that inform the work of competent foreign student advisers.

The fifth chapter catalogues the various areas in which FSA's are well-advised to have some knowledge. Chapter Six treats the skills they will want to develop, and Chapter Seven discusses various aspects of their daily work. Chapter Eight offers some concluding remarks.

References to other publications appear frequently in the *Handbook*. Some of them provide information on rapidly-changing matters such as immigration regulations, on which this *Handbook* is not intended to be an up-to-date reference. Other publications mentioned take FSA's into greater depth than does the *Handbook* on a variety of topics. Competent FSA's have a wide range of interests that is reflected in their reading. Some of the National Association for Foreign Student Affairs (NAFSA) publications cited here should be considered companion volumes to this one. They are available at nominal cost, and they provide essential information and ideas in a number of areas related to foreign student advising.

This *Handbook* is based on one person's experience, judgments, and opinions. Other FSA's might well offer different or even incompatible views. The views set forth here provide a coherent base from which an FSA can function. Readers will want to compare the ideas presented with their own ideas and with those of others who work in the field. The ultimate objective should be the development of outlooks and competencies that somehow provide personal satisfaction, service to higher education, and progress toward the ideal of mutual respect among people with diverse cultural backgrounds.

The
Handbook
of Foreign
Student
Advising

☞1

The Setting

INTEREST IN FOREIGN students[1] in the United States is a relatively recent phenomenon. Until a few years ago, the public, the government, and the faculty and staff of educational institutions paid little mind to students from abroad. Foreign student advisers (FSA's) operated in obscurity, even within their own institutions. The foreign student advising function was often assigned to some person who happened to be available without much thought about what the function entailed or whether the appointee had attitudes, knowledge, or skills suitable for the job.

In the last few years, this situation has changed dramatically. There are many more foreign students in the United States, some of them from countries that have only recently come to exist or to be known to Americans[2] other than specialists. Foreign students are attending all types of U.S. institutions, not just the major universities that enrolled their predecessors. These changes have resulted from a variety of developments at international, national, and institutional levels.

INTERNATIONAL DEVELOPMENTS

Changes in international political and economic relationships, as well as political realignments within individual countries all

[1]Some people prefer the euphemism "international students" to the more precise "foreign students." I prefer the precise term, and use it throughout this volume. My views on this topic are elaborated in "'Foreign' vs. 'International': Can 'International Man' Be Stopped?", which is reproduced in Appendix B.

[2]In the literature about foreign students, the term "American" is often avoided for fear of giving offense to people from Central or South America, who are "Americans" too. Using "North American" or "U.S." as a substitute for "American" often makes for awkward reading. In this *Handbook*, the term "American" is used in the traditional dictionary sense: "of or pertaining to the United States of America."

1

impinge on the work of foreign student advisers. As the United States government becomes more or less active in its alliances with specific foreign countries, the number of students coming from those countries may rise or fall. The development of economic strength in other countries, such as the OPEC nations, Japan or Korea, can bring more foreign students to the U.S. Changes in a particular government's policies can have sudden and dramatic impact on foreign students in the United States. So can "acts of God" such as earthquakes and typhoons. As the number of foreign students and the number of countries they represent grows, there is an increase in the likelihood that some event overseas will affect foreign students, and thus affect FSA's.

NATIONAL DEVELOPMENTS

The U.S. Immigration and Naturalization Service (INS) and a small office in the U.S. Information Agency[3] are no longer the only governmental agencies with a noticeable interest in students from other countries. For a variety of reasons,[4] the Congress, Justice Department personnel outside the INS, the Social Security Administration, and even at times the White House have evinced concern with foreign students.

The national media fairly frequently carry stories about students from other countries, usually to highlight a crisis. *The Chronicle of Higher Education,* widely read among educators, regularly reports on matters concerning international education, and commonly interviews FSA's for articles about students from overseas. Educational associations other than the National Association for Foreign Student Affairs are actively concerned about national and institutional policies affecting students from abroad. This includes disciplinary organizations such as the Engineers Council for Professional Development as well as administrators' organizations such as the American Council on Education and the National Association of State Universities and Land Grant Colleges. Scholars in the area of

[3]The office is currently called the Student Support Services Division, Office of Academic Programs, Bureau of Educational and Cultural Affairs. These names change from time to time.

[4]Factors accounting for the increased attention to foreign students include the growth in their numbers, the so-called "crisis" of Iranian students (see Ahmad Reza Riahinejad's and my article, "Political Depression among Students from Iran"), recruiting abuses by some U.S. educational institutions which attracted foreign enrollees under false pretenses, and the entire issue of "illegal aliens" in the United States.

intercultural communication (e.g., the Brislin and the Samovar, Porter & Jain books cited in the reference list) are recognizing that the work of FSA's is challenging and important.

INSTITUTIONAL DEVELOPMENTS

Today's more numerous foreign students are making their strongest impression in the daily life of the institutions they attend. FSA's are well aware of the increasing demands these students are placing on them. The students are also in daily contact with many others at their institutions—with other foreign students, U.S. students, faculty, student services staff, clerical personnel, and members of the surrounding community.

Of particular interest are the concentrations of students from certain countries (recently, Nigeria, Iran, and Malaysia) and in certain disciplines (recently, engineering and computer science). These concentrations give rise to policy questions concerning the institution's mission, standards, and curriculum. They draw faculty and administrative attention to foreign students, and to foreign student advisers.

In sum, an array of interrelated developments at the international, national, and institutional levels have drawn attention to foreign students and, at least by implication, to foreign student advisers. FSA's now face heavier and more diverse demands for knowledge, thought, sensitivity, and operational effectiveness. If the foreign student population in the United States continues to grow as it has been doing for many years, FSA's will be compelled to modify radically their traditional outlooks and methods of operation. Even now the dominant general ideas or concepts about international educational interchange seem inadequate.

THE CONCEPTUAL SETTING

There are at least two ways in which FSA's are helped by having a clear rationale for their work. First, the solution to many a practical conundrum follows directly from the possession of a clearly conceived general goal. For example, what should an FSA do when asked to advise a sponsored student who wants to marry and remain in the United States rather than honor a contract with a sponsor to return home and teach? There are several possible responses to that question. One would follow from the assumption that the purpose of international educational interchange is to foster economic and social development in countries less prosperous than the United States. Another, and quite different, answer would follow from the assumption that educational interchange is intended to enable individual participants to realize their personal development to the maximum extent possible.

Secondly, a clear rationale helps in the continuing effort to explain oneself and enhance one's own prospects when competing for institutional, state, and national resources and influence. Why should the institution support an FSA? Why should the state not establish policies that discourage foreign students from studying within its borders? Why should U.S. immigration policy be as lenient as possible toward students from abroad? Different answers to these questions flow from different concepts of the nature and purposes of international educational interchange.

Inadequacy of current concepts

Contemporary discussion and debate about foreign students in the United States (and in many other countries as well) is marked by incoherence, inconclusiveness, and a measure of prejudice. Different participants in this discussion—and the same participants at different times—invoke such ideals as enhancing friendship among nations; enhancing understanding among individuals of different nations; developing new markets for U.S. products; favorably influencing future leaders of other countries; promoting "development" in relatively poor countries; aiding the U.S. balance of payments; helping U.S. educational institutions make up for lost domestic enrollment; furthering the personal development of individuals of all nationalities; helping U.S. students learn about other countries; helping all students learn to operate more effectively in intercultural situations; and furnishing educated people in a number of technical fields where Americans are in short supply.

Other participants in this discussion will cite assorted objections to the presence of foreign students in the United States. They point to the additional time and expense foreign students require of institutions; the inclination of some foreign students to remain in the United States following completion of their studies; the perceived misbehavior of some foreign students who express political opinions in ostentatious ways; and the alleged propensity of foreign students to violate U.S. immigration law. People with these views may state or at least imply that foreign students simply do not deserve the privilege of living in the United States, and that people of other nationalities are not intellectually capable of benefiting from educational programs here.

Amidst this plethora of viewpoints, coherent discussion aimed at agreement on policy and practice is unlikely to emerge. The problem, as Josef Mestenhauser puts it, is that the old "paradigm" for international educational interchange no longer serves well, but has yet to be replaced by a new one. Mestenhauser's promising line of thought derives from T.S. Kuhn's analysis of *The Structure of Scientific Revolutions*. Kuhn's general idea, which cannot be discussed at length here, is this: At a given time there prevails a general theory, or concept, or "paradigm" which satisfactorily explains a particular phenomenon or set of phenomena. As knowledge and thought advance, the accepted paradigm is found wanting, and is finally dislodged by a new paradigm that better explains the phenomena in question. One of Kuhn's examples has to do with the replacement of the earth-centered theory of the solar system by the sun-centered theory—the so-called Copernican revolution.

Mestenhauser argues that the current paradigm of international educational interchange developed in the post-World War II era, when (1) the United States was clearly ahead of all other countries in economic and technical strength, (2) foreign students were comparatively few in number, carefully selected, mature, and affiliated with a small number of major U.S. universities, (3) the idea prevailed that all people everywhere would benefit from exposure to U.S. education and technology, (4) it could plausibly be argued that a noticeable portion of foreign students would achieve leadership positions in their countries, and (5) the notion that international person-to-person contacts promoted "world brotherhood" was widely accepted. These circumstances led to the general idea that international educational interchange was a good thing, with political, economic, and humanitarian outcomes which most people regarded favorably.

These circumstances no longer exist, but no new paradigm has arisen from the new circumstances.

Mestenhauser contends that a new concept is needed to lend coherence to contemporary discussion and policy about foreign students. The new concept, he suggests, might have as one of its principle components the notion that foreign students' presence in the United States is needed to help Americans escape their traditional ethnocentricity and learn to function more effectively in a multi-ethnic and interdependent system of countries. Acceptance of that notion would suggest that U.S. institutions, perhaps led by FSA's, might wish to give concerted attention to ways in which foreign and American students can learn from each other and to the development of effective methods for overcoming the barriers that cultural differences erect between them.

Another current notion is that educational interchange allows the United States to attract the intelligent, well-trained people it needs to compete with other countries in high technology fields. Acceptance of that notion would suggest the abandonment of the idea that foreign students "should" in all but exceptional cases return to their own countries after completing their studies.

Yet another issue arises from the fact that in some fields of study foreign students have become integral parts of graduate study and research. Far from being oddities or burdens, foreign students are now indispensable in many engineering, mathematics, computer science, and business departments. The new paradigm will have to acknowledge and accept that fact so that the impulse to ignore, hide or apologize for the presence of foreign students can be overcome. Most foreign students are not in the United States as a result of this country's charity or generosity, but because this country's educational institutions offer something they or their sponsors are willing to pay for, or because the institutions need the foreign students for their own well-being.

Toward a new concept

In their daily lives, FSA's will not be actively involved in the development of a new paradigm for international educational interchange. But, whether they are aware of it or not, policy decisions in their own offices, elsewhere in their institutions, in their states, and in their national capital are being made on the basis of some paradigm or other. FSA's who want to influence those policy decisions cannot ignore the need for a more adequate set of guiding concepts for their work.

☞2

The Nature of the
Foreign Student Adviser Position

THE FOREIGN STUDENT adviser's position is unique. While it is normally at a rather low level in the institutional hierarchy,[1] it demands high levels of knowledge, sensitivity, judgment, tact, and operational effectiveness on the part of its incumbents. It is linked to nearly all parts of the educational institution, and, as we have seen, is highly responsive to contemporary developments elsewhere in the country and around the world. FSA's may be involved in births, marriages, and deaths among their clients, and are often called upon to help foreign students make decisions that have lifelong implications.

To understand the position of the foreign student adviser, we must examine it from a variety of perspectives.

RESPONSIBILITIES

Physicians in the United States graduate from approved schools, are licensed by a state, subscribe to an oath, and belong to a professional association that can censure them for unethical conduct. Given all this, physicians generally have little room to question where their responsibilities lie—to whom and for what they are responsible. While it would be an oversimplification to say they do

---

[1]In their investigation of U.S. college and university policies concerning foreign students, Goodwin & Nacht reported in *Absence of Decision* that "the foreign student adviser was often the least influential figure in the entire organizational structure. Buffeted by events and conscious of impending change in one direction or another, advisers often were powerless to make their views known to higher-level policy makers or to have a voice in the planning process...." The authors go on to say that they "developed a strong sense that in the reconsideration of these issues [about institutional policy concerning foreign students]..., the foreign student adviser is an unusual, well-informed resource who should be used as a catalyst, source of information, and accumulator of campus wisdom far more frequently than is presently the case."

not encounter ethical questions, most of their uncertainties concern
matters of technique.

Not so with FSA's. Lacking mechanisms to assure standardiza-
tion, they have no established answers to the two main questions
about their responsibilities: To whom are they responsible? And,
what are they responsible for doing? (Renwick and Mestenhauser
have written stimulating essays on these issues.) These questions are
easier for physicians to answer not just because the practice of
medicine is more professionalized, but because the physician's job is,
in a sense, simpler. Physicians are supposed to heal or at least com-
fort the sick or afflicted. FSA's face a much greater array of complaints, problems, and issues, and their work gets the attention of an
audience with sharply divergent views as to what FSA's should be
doing.

To whom are FSA's responsible? Different FSA's, in different situations, offer various answers. So do their clients, their supervisors,
and others who observe their work. Among those to whom different
people consider FSA's to be responsible are these:

1. their own consciences, as influenced by their notions of what
   is "good" for international educational interchange, their
   notions of what standards in their field ought to be, their
   personal values, and other factors
2. their supervisors
3. their institutions' chief executive officers
4. the agencies (state or other) that employ them
5. their foreign student clients
6. institutional colleagues
7. colleagues in the field of international educational
   interchange
8. the U.S. Immigration and Naturalization Service
9. agencies that sponsor foreign students
10. the United States government, in general
11. foreign governments, especially those of economically less
    fortunate countries

What are FSA's responsible for doing? Again, there are assorted
answers, given here in no particular order:

1. enforcing U.S. immigration law and regulations
2. assuring that foreign students behave decorously

3. handling crises involving foreign students

4. helping foreign students adjust to a new culture

5. helping foreign students realize their educational objectives with the least possible difficulty

6. relieving institutional colleagues of the burden of dealing with students from abroad

7. helping institutional colleagues deal with students from abroad

8. monitoring foreign students' academic and perhaps social conduct on behalf of sponsoring agencies and/or foreign governments

9. helping U.S. students, staff, faculty, and/or community members learn from foreign students about other societies and/or about intercultural relationships

10. helping foreign students achieve the maximum feasible amount of self-development

11. helping poorer countries develop

The various answers to the two questions about responsibilities are sometimes complementary, but can be incompatible. FSA's are well-advised to review these answers and note those (or others not listed here) which most closely approximate the ones to which they themselves adhere. More specific ideas about choosing from among them appear in Chapter Four. Meanwhile, we will look at the FSA position as it is viewed by certain other groups of people.

THE FSA POSITION AS VIEWED BY OTHERS

The occupant of any role is influenced by, among other things, other people's perceptions of the role and of the person who occupies it. FSA's are constrained by their image in the eyes of foreign students, institutional colleagues, and external agencies.

Foreign student views

Foreign students' perceptions (or conceptions) of the FSA are strongly influenced by their past experience with employees of organizations ("bureaucracies") and by the experience they and their friends have had with particular foreign student advisers. At one extreme is the view that the FSA is an agent of intelligence or law enforcement organizations. This conception is commonly found among students from countries where a centralized government uses police and informants to monitor the behavior of citizens and guard against "disloyal" conduct. Foreign students who come to the United States from countries of this type, and many do, find it difficult to believe that American educational institutions employ people simply to assist foreign students in attaining their educational goals. Ties to the INS, the FBI, the CIA, and perhaps other countries' national intelligence agencies are assumed to exist. I have long since given up trying to dissuade students who hold this view. Their preconceptions are too strong to overcome.

At the other extreme are those students who view the FSA's as utterly benevolent figures who can and will resolve any difficulty the students face. These students, in contrast to those discussed in the preceding paragraph, are likely to visit their FSA's with considerable frequency.

Between these extremes is a continuum of views on the matter of foreign student advisers' loyalties and abilities. Wherever their views fit on this continuum, foreign students, for reasons discussed in a moment, are likely to overestimate the amount of power FSA's possess. FSA's are well-advised to try to assess the conceptions of their role and competence that prevail among the foreign students on their particular campuses.

Institutional colleagues' views

Faculty and staff perceptions of FSA's are most strongly influenced by their own attitudes toward foreign students and by the FSA's reputation for competence. If a new FSA assumes office after another person has held the position for a number of years, the predecessor's reputation and image are likely to influence institutional colleagues' perceptions of the FSA's role and responsibilities for a considerable period. This can be a problem for the new FSA if the predecessor was held in either unusually high or unusually low regard. The new FSA may disappoint colleagues who have come to expect a consistently outstanding performance from the foreign student adviser, or encounter resistance if the predecessor was deemed ineffective or misguided.

Faculty and staff who are favorably inclined toward foreign students are likely to have a positive view of FSA's, or at least to give them the benefit of the doubt. The opposite is true of faculty and staff who are unfavorably disposed toward students from other countries.

The FSA's place in the institutional structure is another factor that influences colleagues' perceptions of the FSA's role. Many FSA's are in the student affairs branch of the administration. While at some institutions student affairs personnel are generally held in high regard, at others they are not. An FSA's effectiveness can be affected by the general image of the part of the institutional structure in which the FSA position is located, and by the amount of power and influence (these terms are discussed below) the FSA's superior holds within the organization.

It is mainly through competent performance, however, that FSA's can enhance their influence among institutional colleagues. The subject of an FSA's influence is discussed at greater length later.

External agencies' views

FSA's deal with so many external agencies that it is nearly impossible to generalize about the agencies' views of them. The agencies include the INS and other federal bodies, sponsoring organizations, the education sections of foreign embassies, and assorted community organizations. Their perceptions of FSA's are shaped by, among other things, individual staff members' attitudes toward foreign students, the agency's corporate experience with FSA's, and the nature of the agency's business with foreign student advisers.

It is probably safe to say that INS staff members generally regard most FSA's as being soft-hearted and amateurish, or at least as inadequately devoted to upholding the immigration law. The staff members of sponsoring agencies and of embassies probably have a more differentiated view of FSA's, depending on their experience with different individuals who fill that role. Some FSA's are seen as helpful, well-informed, and reasonable; some are seen as negligent or even hostile toward their foreign student clients; still others are seen as excessively paternalistic (or maternalistic) in their outlooks.

Community organizations' perceptions of FSA's vary widely, depending on the viewpoints of the various individuals involved and on the history of the interactions between the FSA's and the organizations. Some FSA's are seen as competent, helpful, and willing or even eager to cooperate. Others are viewed less positively.

Even FSA's hold diverse views about how foreign student advisers are supposed to operate.

THE FSA POSITION AS SEEN BY FSA's THEMSELVES

At one institution I visited as a consultant, I was talking with a faculty member about the foreign student situation there. "The foreign students here won't blow their noses without checking with Alice" (not the FSA's real name), he told me. Discussion with several foreign students at the institution indicated that the faculty member was exaggerating only slightly. Alice reserved residence hall rooms for new foreign students, selected their roommates, and made sure their relationships with their roommates were harmonious. She helped them open their bank accounts and made sure they kept their check registers accurately. They received their mail through her office. She served as their academic adviser, and if they had problems in any of their classes she would intercede with the teacher on their behalf. The students seemed to have unbounded respect and affection for Alice. Her institutional colleagues seemed to respect her too, although sometimes grudgingly.

I have visited other institutions where some of the foreign students were not certain who the foreign student adviser was.

And there are still other institutions where all the foreign students know who the FSA is, but, as one faculty member said, "No one goes there (to the FSA's office) except to get signatures on immigration forms." Not all FSA's are as well known or as beloved as Alice.

FSA's vary in the degree to which they become involved in the lives of foreign students. There is variation, too, in the manner in which they become involved. Some FSA's take a *laissez-faire* or very non-directive approach. Some are moderately directive. Some, like Alice, are maternalistic. And some are quite authoritarian. One FSA, for example, told a foreign student to stop signing petitions on political issues or the FSA would report him to the INS and have him deported. That same FSA told another foreign student to either stop dating native[2] women or never again enter the institution's international center.

---

[2]From the viewpoint of foreign students, the people among whom they live are "natives." I think it is helpful to use that term from time to time to remind us about how others see us, and to remind us also of the power of particular words to evoke certain viewpoints and images.

Within certain constraints, the FSA's personality seems to be the principle variable affecting the way the task of foreign student advising is approached. Those constraints include the size and type of the institution, the number and academic level of the foreign students, and the ratio between the number of foreign students and the number of FSA's. Had Alice worked at an institution with several hundred foreign students instead of several dozen, for example, she could not have assumed so active a role in their lives. English language students tend to need more FSA attention than other foreign students do, and undergraduates more than graduates.

Among the personality characteristics influencing the manner in which FSA's approach their work, the need to exercise power seems quite important. Some people have a strong need to dominate others, while other people have little or no such need. Foreign students are often susceptible to domination, especially when they are new to the country, because they have limited information and few if any social contacts. The FSA is the "natural" source of information and guidance, and in that role can often manipulate or control the students. Some FSA's seem to train foreign students to be dependent on them, thus fulfilling their desire to be in control of other people.

Other personality characteristics influencing an FSA's approach to foreign students include the capacity to empathize, degree of judgmentalness, strength of the need to be liked, and degree of respect for other people. Some of these and other personality characteristics are the subject of Chapter Three.

Let me offer here an analysis of the position of the foreign student adviser. As we have seen, this subject is value-laden. So the analysis will inevitably be prescriptive. Others in the field might offer different prescriptions.

AN ANALYSIS OF THE FSA POSITION

We have already observed that the FSA position normally occupies a rather low position in the institutional hierarchy. Some FSA's are deans or directors, but most are not. Most FSA's have little power. They may, however, have considerable influence. An understanding of the concepts of power and influence is important to an understanding of the FSA position, so the next several paragraphs will be devoted to those concepts as they pertain to FSA's.

Power and influence

Definitions.   Power is customarily defined or described as the ability to induce others to behave in certain ways through the dispensation of rewards or punishments. Power in an institutional setting arises from control over resources (money, mainly, and sometimes information) that are in short supply, and from occupancy of roles officially vested with authority. The more powerful positions in an organization are the higher level ones whose occupants dispense jobs and money. They establish mission statements, institutional policies, and job descriptions for lower level employees.

In an institution, then, power is based mainly on position in the hierarchy.

Influence, by contrast, is the ability to induce others to behave in certain ways by other means than the dispensation of rewards or punishments or the exercise of formal authority. A powerful person may or may not be influential; a person without power may have considerable influence. Influence can arise from many things, including recognized competence, articulateness, intelligence, knowledgeability, informal relationships with powerful or influential people, a record of accomplishment in some respected undertaking, sociability, and physical attractiveness.

FSA's and power.   Most FSA's have little if any power. They can give or withhold signatures on immigration forms (a power which some FSA's use to induce foreign students to behave or not behave in certain ways), but otherwise they are rarely in a position to work their will through the dispensation of rewards or punishments. Unless they are deans or directors (and sometimes even if they are), they are not high in the chain of command. They rarely have the authority to allocate funds in any significant amount or to control jobs other than clerical ones. They usually cannot assign residence hall rooms, design courses that suit foreign student interests, or offer academic credit to induce students to participate in programs they might organize. At smaller institutions, the FSA responsibility may be only one of many vested in an already overworked administrator. If such people have power in their institutions, it is usually because one or more of their other responsibilities holds higher status within the hierarchy. Their power is likely to be in their own chain of command only, however, and not in other parts of the institution.

The fact that FSA's have little power is not obvious to everyone. Foreign students, in particular, are generally unfamiliar with North American-style bureaucracies and their job descriptions, chains of command, and emphasis on "objective" decision-making. Foreign students are likely to interact more with the FSA than with any other member of the administration. They know the FSA has some relationship with immigration regulations and procedures. From all this foreign students may erroneously infer that FSA's have more power than they actually do.

FSA's are, in fact, best viewed as *intermediaries*, people who, while lacking power, work to bring different people together in the pursuit of common aims. To function effectively, intermediaries need influence.

FSA's and influence.   While they usually lack power, FSA's may have influence. They may therefore be able to accomplish a good deal on behalf of their clients even though their formal status in the hierarchy is not high. We have already listed factors which contribute to influence. Let us list them again, because they deserve careful attention. In the absence of real possibilities for obtaining power, FSA's who want to be effective need to work consciously and conscientiously at enhancing their influence. That means paying attention to these factors:

1. acknowledged competence
2. articulateness
3. intelligence
4. knowledgeability
5. informal relationships with powerful or influential people
6. sociability
7. a record of accomplishment in some respected undertaking
8. physical attractiveness

Many of these factors will receive further consideration later in the *Handbook*. The point to be stressed here is that an FSA's effectiveness is usually much more a function of influence than of power. Influence, of course, is not a physical entity. It is subjective and is therefore perceived differently by different people. This fact produces one of the most interesting aspects of the FSA position—its many audiences.

The FSA's numerous audiences

When we raised the question, "To whom is the FSA responsible?" we saw that there were many possible answers. The effective FSA has influence among foreign student clients, faculty and staff throughout the institution, INS officials, the personnel of sponsoring agencies, people in the community, and probably other FSA's. The problem is that an action which may raise an FSA's stature in the eyes of one of these audiences may diminish it in the eyes of another. Some FSA's, for example, will take the position of advocate for virtually any foreign student who is in any sort of difficulty, no matter how irresponsible or even devious the student may have been. Such an FSA might be held in high regard by foreign students, but is unlikely to hold the faculty's respect or that of district INS personnel.

Other FSA's are considered by foreign students at their institutions to be suspicious of most foreign students, skeptical about their motives and mistrustful of what they say. Such FSA's cannot hope to have influence with their foreign student clients.

These are extreme, although not unusual, examples. The point remains that FSA's, like everyone else, cannot please all of the people all of the time.

The balancing act

Faced with diverse and sometimes incompatible expectations and standards of evaluation, FSA's must continually seek a balance among competing wishes, interests, demands, and viewpoints. This implies taking all pertinent viewpoints into account, and then applying defensible standards to the making of a judgment. This is the essence of a foreign student adviser's job. Those who do it well will gain the respect of their various audiences and will accrue influence among them. Those who act on the basis of inadequate information, faulty assumptions, or inappropriate standards will lose respect and influence.

The so-called "Iranian student crisis" of the late 1970's and early 1980's presented many foreign student advisers with extreme challenges to their ability to maintain a balance. When Iranian students began coming to the United States in large numbers in the second half of the 1970's, they were not especially popular on many campuses or in many communities. They were seen as aggressive, hypocritically obsequious, and untrustworthy. FSA's who seemed sympathetic to them risked incurring the disrespect of their institutional colleagues. As the "revolution" progressed in Iran, some Iranian students participated in political demonstrations that sometimes became violent, and the reputation of Iranian students and FSA's who seemed to sympathize with them suffered further.

Then came periods in which funds from Iran were cut off. Some Iranian students had enough savings to see them through; others did not. Many of the latter turned to their FSA's for help. These FSA's knew it was their job to try to help these foreign students who were in financial difficulty due to circumstances beyond their control, but the students were widely disliked and resented. FSA's were caught in the middle. How far could they go in trying to help these students?

The taking of the American hostages in Tehran evoked strong anti-Iranian sentiments throughout the United States. Iranian students here were sometimes victims of hostile acts. They began, on the other hand, to gain the sympathy of some FSA's and others who saw them as victims, as people being punished for an action in which they had no role. FSA's were again caught between their wish to assist their clients and public hostility toward those clients.

Then the U.S. government, through the Immigration and Naturalization Service, set out to identify and interview all Iranian students in the country. Many INS district offices sought educational institutions' cooperation in this undertaking, usually by asking FSA's to aid in arranging the interviews. This caught FSA's between their need to retain reasonable working relationships with the INS and their desire to show some allegiance to their students. Should they cooperate with the INS? If so, to what extent? What could they do to provide Iranian students with the documents they needed for the interviews?

When the Khomeini regime took over in Iran and instituted sweeping restrictions on the remission of dollars abroad, FSA's on many campuses were faced with needy students on the one hand and tight budgets and sometimes unsympathetic institutional colleagues on the other. How far could they press the students' case? Many of the students did not want to return to Iran, given what they perceived to be the repressive and anti-intellectual nature of the

Khomeini government. But the U.S. government was generally not sympathetic with this attitude. What were FSA's to do?

Volumes could no doubt be written about the manner in which the Iranian student crisis was handled on different campuses. These volumes would show FSA's ever in the middle, caught among competing and incompatible pressures, hopes, demands, and expectations. Some FSA's emerged with heightened influence. Others were less able to find a workable balance and their influence declined.

The Iranian student crisis was no doubt an extreme case, given its duration, the strong emotions it evoked, and the large number of students involved. But FSA's can expect to encounter more and more situations requiring delicate balances as long as the number of foreign students in the United States remains large and conditions within and among so many countries remain volatile.

The use of influence: FSA's as leaders

FSA's have a comprehensive view of their institutions' foreign student-related policies and procedures. They can see when foreign students suffer from deficiencies in the preparation and distribution of pre-arrival information, in the orientation program, in housing policies, in financial aid arrangements, in academic advising, and so on. While they may see things that need to be changed, FSA's usually lack the power to bring about changes through their own efforts alone. If they want to improve the foreign student programs at their institutions, FSA's need to assume a leadership role and develop the influence needed for effective leadership.

What has been said here about the FSA's position is rather theoretical. Some more practical observations come in Chapter Four, under the heading of "Role of the FSA."

☞3

Personal Characteristics

IN A POSITION such as that of a for-
eign student adviser, where so much more is required than the
mechanical application of certain standards or procedures, the personal characteristics of the incumbent assume considerable importance. There are ten characteristics that, in my judgment, are
necessary for effective functioning as an FSA. Those characteristics
are intelligence, patience, nonjudgmentalness, interest in cultural
differences, respect for others, tolerance for ambiguity, sociability,
self-awareness, kindness, and decisiveness.

It is, of course, rather arbitrary to select these ten characteristics.
Another person might choose a different set or make a longer or
shorter list. In discussing these characteristics I will try to explain
why they were considered to be especially important to FSA's, and
how some of them might be cultivated.

INTELLIGENCE

It is not the purpose here to enter into the debate about the
meaning of "intelligence," or of any of the other concepts on this
list. The term intelligence, as used here, refers to several qualities:
the ability to retain large amounts of information; the ability to
discern relationships among various ideas, facts, or events; the ability to solve problems; the ability to reason clearly.

FSA's encounter a wide variety of personalities, situations, and
kinds of problems. Being able to apply extensive knowledge in constructive and creative ways is clearly an asset to them. Intelligence,
too, contributes to influence. Other things being equal, a more intelligent person will have more success as an FSA than a less intelligent

19

person will. While intelligence itself (whatever it is) may not readily be fostered in an adult, some habits of mind closely related to intelligence can be promoted. These include exposing oneself to a wide range of information, learning to focus attention, and exercising self-discipline in the pursuit of solutions to problems.

PATIENCE

It is sometimes harder for FSA's to be patient with fellow Americans than with foreign students. An American FSA expects to have to maintain a pleasant disposition in interactions with people from abroad whose English proficiency is limited and whose backgrounds have not prepared them to understand local customs, institutions, and techniques. An FSA is the target of many "simple" questions from foreign students, and may have to work long and hard to make the reply understood. It is easy to understand why this is so. Remaining patient is simply part of the job.

Some of the questions and comments of one's fellow Americans are harder to endure with equanimity. "Do you speak all their languages?" I have been asked countless times. (That would be 30 or 40 languages.) "Don't they all have a lot of money?" (Some do and some do not; I have known some who could afford to eat but once a day.) Since it is one of the FSA's tasks to enhance institutional and community receptivity to foreign students, the Americans' naive questions and sometimes offensive stereotypes (about foreign students' body odors, for example) are best treated with patience and forbearance.

Impatience is rarely a constructive quality in human relationships. Most people know when they are becoming impatient. Accelerated breathing, heartbeat, and speech are the common symptoms. People who want to be more patient (or who have been persuaded that more patience would be valuable, whether they want to be patient or not), can learn to be aware of these symptoms and to pause, or momentarily withdraw, when they appear.

NONJUDGMENTALNESS

Most students of intercultural (and other interpersonal) relations include nonjudgmentalness on their list of characteristics necessary for functioning constructively in intercultural situations. "Things in the other culture are not right or wrong," the cliche goes, "they are just different."

Long before we become interested in intercultural relations we are advised not to be judgmental. "Judge not, lest ye be judged," says an admonition from a highly respected source. "Let the one who has not sinned cast the first stone," says another. And, with an intercultural bent, "Do not judge another man until you have walked a mile in his moccasins."

The validity of these warnings is reinforced by our own experience with judgmentalness in others. We try to avoid people who we know will judge or evaluate us. If we cannot avoid their presence, we avoid discussion topics we suppose will evoke their judgments of us. And we know how much we welcome the presence of people who do not judge us, people who accept us as we are and do not convey the idea that we ought somehow to be different in order to have their approval. We can relax in the presence of such people, and speak as we wish about what we will, without fear.

Yet nonjudgmental people are rare. Most of us emerge from childhood with our heads filled with "shoulds" about other people's ideas and behavior. When other people fail to act the way they "should," as they inevitably do, we judge them negatively. FSA's had better work against this tendency to evaluate others because it is in no way constructive and because their clients, having been raised with sometimes radically different ideas, will frequently behave in ways that will force FSA's to disapprove if they insist on judging. As James Bostain of the Foreign Service Institute puts it in one of his lectures, "People act the way they are taught to act, and they all have different teachers."

It is far easier to agree that judging others is a negative behavior than it is to stop judging them. To stop judging, one has to convince oneself *completely* that *it is not necessary to judge others*. To put it another way, and to relate it to the topic of the *Handbook*, FSA's do not need to have an opinion about how foreign students should be and what they should do. FSA's might have well-founded views about the likely outcomes of certain of their clients' attitudes and behaviors, and they can certainly describe those views to their clients. But they need make no judgments of other people's value as human beings. To the degree that they can rid themselves of "shoulds" and accept others as they are, they will become more approachable, more respected, and more effective.

None of this is to say that FSA's are not expected to make judgments of any kind. Of course they are, but with respect to their own and others' behavior, not with respect to other people's value as human beings.

A fruitful way to help foreign students learn to reduce judgmentalism, and thereby help them function better in their intercultural interactions, is the "D.I.E. Formulation," described in Appendix C.

INTEREST IN CULTURAL DIFFERENCES

One of the fascinations of foreign student advising is seeing the manifold ways in which cultural backgrounds affect people's ideas and behavior. Beyond that is the interplay of cultures as foreign students interact with each other and with the natives. FSA's work in a living laboratory for studying intercultural relations, and those who are interested in that topic will encounter an endless supply of incidents about which to think, write, and teach others. An example is an article called "The Intercultural Meeting," reproduced in Appendix D.

People who are not interested in the subject of cultural differences and intercultural relations, or who consider cultural differences to be inconveniences and impediments to the proper functioning of things, are not likely to enjoy working as FSA's. Some FSA's seem interested in cultural differences, but only insofar as they produce examples of quaint or novel human conduct. People with this outlook usually behave in a condescending way toward foreign students. Foreign students sense that, of course, and respond negatively.

It is not just for reasons of personal or professional satisfaction that FSA's are advised to have an intense interest in cultural differences. It is also because so much of their work entails helping foreign students and members of the host institution and community understand cultural differences and cope with their effects. Whether through orientation or other types of educational programs, workshops, public speaking, advising and counseling, general problem-solving, or the preparation of written materials, FSA's are trying to help others understand how cultures shape people's ideas and behavior, and how cultural differences can be confronted constructively.

RESPECT FOR OTHERS

To say that FSA's had better have a respectful attitude toward other people may seem redundant, since related points have already been made. Yet the topic deserves some specific treatment.

Respecting other people requires a constant struggle against the tendency to evaluate others and to see our own behavior as natural and others' as unnatural. We might acknowledge the importance of feeling and displaying respect for others, and we may feel and display such respect on most occasions, but there are always situations in which true respect does not seem to be present. Often these situations have to do with male-female relations (e.g., the custom of arranged marriages and the manner in which many Middle Eastern and African men treat women—including their own wives) or with status relationships (for example, Oriental formality toward older or higher status people). Our ideas about male-female relationships and relationships among people of different statuses are so deeply set that respecting diverse ideas about those relationships requires constant and concerted effort.

The other point to be made here is that respecting differences among Americans is often more difficult than respecting differences manifested by people from other cultures.

People who are generally open-minded and accepting of cultural differences reflected among foreign students may become self-righteous and intolerant in their responses to institutional colleagues whom they regard as racist, sexist, or chauvinistic. The psychodynamic roots of the foreign students' and the institutional colleagues' values and attitudes may be identical, but the former may be accorded respect and the latter not. It sometimes seems to be easier for human beings to accept others who are comprehensively different from themselves than to accept others who resemble them in many ways but are different in some others. Our institutional colleagues "should" think and act properly (that is, the way we do), we seem to tell ourselves.

FSA's need to be able to work constructively with colleagues throughout their institutions, so they need to challenge any tendency they find in themselves to judge and condemn colleagues with different values and viewpoints.

TOLERANCE FOR AMBIGUITY

An ambiguous situation, we can say, is one lacking a clear genesis, a set of boundaries, a set of cues for expected behavior, and/or an anticipated outcome. In an ambiguous situation, one cannot be certain what is happening or how one ought to behave. Ambiguous situations frequently occur in intercultural relationships, tending to promote anxiety and feelings of insecurity.

Some people have a low tolerance for ambiguity. They insist, at a psychological level, on explicitness and clarity. They react with impatience and sometimes anger when things are not made clear for them; they may supply their own clarity by closing out alternative explanations and insisting that they know *the* true nature of a situation.

Because FSA's are working with people who have diverse world views, values, and assumptions, they will inevitably become involved in ambiguous situations. I well remember, for example, an agitated student coming to me and insisting that I help resolve a problem that involved him and his wife and child, on the one hand, and another couple who lived in the same apartment complex, on the other. According to the student, his infant son was persistently ill because the woman in the other couple was practicing witchcraft on him. It was my job, the student said, to right this wrong.

Unless one knows right away how to handle interfamily conflicts centered on witchcraft, a situation such as this is, from the FSA's view, an ambiguous one. What is really happening? Indeed, how can one even find out what is happening? What is one to do? What possible resolutions exist? Only with patience and respect can one proceed to inquire into the various participants' views of the situation, their own suggestions about solutions, and eventual mediation.

In the particular situation offered as an example here, the mediation was not successful. A first mediation session did produce an agreement that the disputants would avoid each other and try to prevent any escalation of their conflict. The agreement held for several months. Then it broke down and another session became necessary. That session ended in a screaming, hitting, scratching melee that five campus security officers came to quell. The conflict between the families was never resolved. It dissipated when the students graduated and moved away. I never did understand what was happening. I think FSA's encounter many situations that are beyond their comprehension, situations where they do not know and will never know what is happening. The case study in Appendix A is another example. An FSA will want to be able to respond to these ambiguous situations with patience and with a willingness to be involved despite the lack of clarity and the absence of guidelines for conduct.

Signs of intolerance with ambiguous situations combine the signs of impatience—accelerated breathing, heartbeat, and speech—with a spoken or unspoken insistence that the situation has certain specific characteristics. "What is at issue here is thus-and-so," for example, or "If Person X would only do or understand such-and-such, everything would be fine." Another sign of intolerance with ambiguity is a feeling of uncertainty about what one's own role in a situation ought to be, coupled with a feeling of discomfort resulting from that uncertainty.

Upon recognizing these signs an FSA can pause and say (internally), "This is one of those ambiguous situations I will inevitably encounter. I need to be patient, try to understand it better, and recognize that I may never understand it at all."

SOCIABILITY

Richard Brislin[1] makes these interesting comments on the idea of sociability:

> Some people are warm, make others feel comfortable in their presence through choice of topics in conversation, are able to communicate an interest in people, and are considerate enough to listen to others rather than to talk at them. Related traits are respect for others with different points of view, an interest in topics to which a person may not have been exposed but which are important to others, a willingness to sacrifice one's own desires in favor of someone else's (selflessness), and an

[1]Brislin's *Cross-Cultural Encounters* supplies numerous ideas and suggestions that are stimulating and helpful for FSA's and others who work with people from different cultures. I think it would be good for everyone who works with foreign students to read *Cross-Cultural Encounters* twice. The quotation cited here is from page 59.

ability to be nonjudgmental when observing unfamiliar behaviors or hearing different opinions.

This definition contains many elements already discussed. Brislin includes sociability among the variables he says influence a person's success in intercultural situations.

Certainly sociability is an asset to FSA's, not just in their dealings with foreign students but also in their interactions with institutional and professional colleagues, agency representatives, and members of the community. Encounters with foreigners or strangers can be uncomfortable because of a lack of agreement as to what discussion topics and styles of interaction (see Barnlund's comparison of American and Japanese communicative styles) are appropriate. A sociable person can reduce this discomfort and help people find a satisfactory means of relating.

SELF-AWARENESS

FSA's can benefit from self-awareness on both the cultural and personal levels.

From the viewpoint of their foreign student clients, FSA's (unless they are natives of other countries) are sample Americans. FSA's need to know what it is about them that their clients are likely to consider exemplary of the local culture.

And FSA's will have countless occasions to explain aspects of the local culture to foreign students. For this reason, too, an awareness of the culturally-based aspects of their own ideas and responses is beneficial. The characteristics of "American culture" that seem to draw the most consistent attention of foreign students are the emphasis on the individual, informality in interpersonal relationships, and the action orientation. On these and related topics, FSA's will want to digest Edward Stewart's *American Cultural Patterns: A Cross-Cultural Perspective.* A useful, brief summary of American cultural characteristics can also be found in Samovar, Porter, & Jain's *Understanding Intercultural Communication.*

In addition to these readings FSA's can gain cultural self-awareness by means of conversations with foreign students. Their observations about American society can be most instructive.

Personal self-awareness cannot come from books as readily as cultural self-awareness can. It is more likely to come from introspection and from hearing other people's relatively uninhibited responses to one's ideas and behavior. It is an interesting commentary on North American society that many people here do not have friends or acquaintances who are willing to tell them openly and freely what sort of impression they are making, what their nonverbal behavior reveals about their feelings, what their characteristic responses to typical situations are, how they might improve aspects of their behavior toward other people, and other such personal matters.[2] To get this "feedback," as it is termed in the jargon of counseling, Americans may be compelled to join some sort of "encounter group" or "sensitivity training program," or take a course in group dynamics or interpersonal communication.

If joining a group or taking a course is what FSA's must do in order to gain some self-insight and some perspective on the way they seem to others, then they ought to join a group or take a course. FSA's, like other people who do counseling and advising or in any other way try to help other people on a personal level, will want to have a significant measure of self-awareness. They will want to be able to answer such questions about themselves as the following:

1. What sort of impression do I make on most other people?

2. How do others' perceptions of me jibe with my perceptions of myself?

3. How am I feeling right now? (Asked at any given time.)

4. What is happening in this conversation right now? (Asked at any given time.)

5. What topics or situations do I typically handle less well than I would like?

6. What typical behaviors of mine are commonly misconstrued by others?

7. What typical behaviors of others do I commonly misconstrue?

8. What are my strengths and weaknesses in dealing with situations that involve tension? Anger? Conflict?

[2]Americans seem to have the idea they they should not tell their friends negative things about them because it will "hurt their feelings." In some other societies, people *will* tell their friends negative things about them because they believe their friends need to know them and will not hear them from anyone else. Americans, it seems to me, often have no one who will tell them things they most need to know about themselves.

9. Do I commonly make unwarranted assumptions about other people?
10. What are my prejudices about other people?
11. What modifications in my outlook and behavior might make me more able to contribute constructively in the human situations of which I am a part?

Effective FSA's are self-aware enough to have answers to questions such as these and to be able to keep such questions at some accessible level of consciousness during most of their interactions with others. This self-awareness enables FSA's to monitor their interactions as they take place, and to modify their approaches when modifications seem necessary to keep the interaction constructive.

KINDNESS

Kindness, we can say, complements what Carl Rogers calls "unconditional positive regard," which is a combination of positive feelings and expectations about other human beings. Kindness also implies concern, empathy, and caring.

FSA's are often called upon to help people. They also see many situations in which people could use help whether they seek it or not. Foreigners anywhere often need help because there is, by definition, so much they do not know about the local scene. It is not just foreign students who can use an FSA's help, however, but also local people who interact with foreign students. This might include U.S. students, faculty, institutional staff, landlords and landladies, merchants, the local police, and many others. Effective FSA's are the sort of people who have a natural impulse to help others.[3] Their kindness is reflected not just in actions they might take to ameliorate unpleasant situations, but also in the respectful and sympathetic way they respond in conversations with others.

DECISIVENESS

My colleague Martin Limbird, who works in an international education office, often gives this response when asked about his occupation: "My job is to change the world." That is a big job, of course. People with such big jobs always have more than enough

[3]As we will see in the next chapter, under the heading of "problem ownership," there are limits on the help an effective FSA will offer.

work to do. Effective FSA's are nearly always very busy because they have many demands on them and so many things they want to accomplish.

People who want to accomplish a great deal benefit from being decisive. Decisive people are those who recognize that decisions need to be made, that many decisions must be made on the basis of inadequate information, that most choices have both positive and negative consequences (often unforeseen and unforeseeable), that the negative consequences of most decisions can be endured, and that most decisions, if their outcomes turn out to be unacceptable, can be changed.

Having all these premises in mind, decisive people, once they have gathered what pertinent information they can and reflected on it for a reasonable amount of time, make their decisions and move on.

Decisiveness is a characteristic that can be cultivated. Fostering it mainly entails convincing oneself of the validity of the premises given above. Albert Ellis's chapter on "Enhancing Decisiveness" in *Executive Leadership: A Rational Approach* offers useful suggestions to people who would like to get more accomplished by reducing their tendency to postpone the making of decisions.

☞ 4

Attitudes and Ideas

PEOPLE WHO WORK with people approach their jobs with one or another set of ideas and attitudes concerning their clients and their own role *vis-a-vis* those clients. That set of attitudes and ideas shapes the way in which they carry out their responsibilities. It helps them decide what situations they should enter, how they should treat other people, what outcomes they should seek, and what actions are and are not appropriate, moral, or ethical.

This chapter examines some of the attitudes and ideas FSA's bring to their work.

CONCEPTIONS OF FOREIGN STUDENTS

In the early 1970's the National Association for Foreign Student Affairs (NAFSA), like many other U.S. organizations, was divided by a debate about student participation in its meetings and other activities. Proponents of student participation argued that people who worked with students had an obligation to hear directly from those students about their perceived needs, wishes, and interests.

One opponent of student participation in NAFSA said, "When you've heard one foreign student, you've heard them all." This statement captures one extreme view of foreign students that can be found among FSA's. According to this view, foreign students are all alike in their image of themselves as favored beings, their insistence on special treatment at the hands of the institutions they attend, their self-righteousness, and their intention to thwart the true objectives of "educational exchange" by settling permanently in the United States.

The other extreme view holds that foreign students are noble and heroic, always right, and deserving of reverence, close attention, and special treatment of many kinds.

Most foreign student advisers' conceptions of their clients are more differentiated than either of these extremes, and are more moderate. Whatever those conceptions are, they will influence the manner in which FSA's receive their clients, the way they treat them, and the lengths to which they will go to serve them.

The ideal is probably to strive to see each student as an individual, recognizing that generalizations can be made about people from particular cultures, but that any student might be an exception to any of those generalizations. Dennis Peterson, for example, points out that Middle Eastern students may diverge from the generalizations or stereotypes FSA's and others might have about people from their area of the world. He says a particular Middle Eastern student might not be a typical person even in his own country, or may have internalized much from U.S. culture, or may have adopted attitudes and behaviors that combine elements from his own and U.S. culture. These possibilities exist for students from any part of the world, of course, not just Middle Easterners.

Richard Brislin believes FSA's will almost inevitably succumb to stereotyping foreign students, given the pressure under which they typically work and the large numbers of students with whom they come into contact. This tendency is more likely to be evident at large institutions than at small ones, it seems to me.

If FSA's can treat students as individuals, they can make independent assessments of each client's motivations, intentions, reliability, and so on, rather than operating on the basis of unwarranted generalizations. In doing so, they will be showing the respect that, as mentioned above, is an important component of success in foreign student advising.

It is not enough to urge that FSA's strive to treat their clients as individuals rather than as members of stereotyped groups. Even if stereotypes about specific nationalities are avoided (which is probably not entirely possible) or at least held consciously and frequently reexamined (which is possible), there remain the feelings most Americans harbor about foreigners in general. That topic needs some comment.

As they grow up, people in the United States are continually exposed to the idea that theirs is a superior country and way of life. (The Japanese and some others are taught this idea too, but people in many countries are not.) Foreigners (except maybe Canadians and, in some cases, Europeans) come to be seen as somehow less human and less intelligent than people in the United States, less able to solve life's problems and less emotionally complex than "real" people such as ourselves.

One important product of this assumption, as it is manifested in dealings with foreign students, is somewhat paradoxical. On the one hand there is an expectation that foreign students, exempt as they are from complexity in thought, feeling, and motivation, should be better than domestic students. They should get good grades, speak English well, and behave nicely at all times. (This idea is elaborated in an article called "Foreign Students and Double Standards," reproduced in Appendix E.)

On the other hand, foreign students in the United States are very often treated in a patronizing way. It is not unusual to hear foreign students being discussed or gossiped about in tones like those used to discuss children. They are frequently spoken to in the manner that children are; they may be considered not to need or deserve confidentiality of treatment or the procedural protections that U.S. students routinely receive. The assumption is commonly made that all students from a particular country will know and like each other and will willingly give and receive help from each other. There is also a common assumption that foreign students who are members of a particular family (sisters, cousins, etc.) will have harmonious relationships. These are not assumptions we make about ourselves, however. It would be considered ridiculous to suppose that all Americans will like each other just because they happen to be compatriots, or that all family relationships among them are harmonious.

Given their upbringing, it is extremely difficult for most people in the United States to learn to see foreign students, and other foreigners, as individuals worthy of unqualified respect. I believe that the subtle feeling that foreigners are inferior persists even among FSA's; it certainly persists among institutional colleagues and in our communities. Those who doubt the existence of these feelings need only ask some foreign students whether they think most Americans treat them as individuals who deserve respect.

THE ROLE OF THE FOREIGN STUDENT ADVISER

I argued in Chapter Two that FSA's have little or no power in most of their dealings and must cultivate influence in order to be effective. I went on to take the position that this influence will be enhanced to the degree that FSA's can find an appropriate balance in meeting the various responsibilities and expectations they face. I will now offer some more specific ideas about the FSA's role. These ideas are presented with the knowledge that reasonable people can have differing opinions on this topic. I will begin with a description of a minimal set of responsibilities for an FSA, and then discuss some additional responsibilities.

Various job descriptions

Minimal FSA responsibilities. A minimal job description for an FSA is probably "to provide foreign students with assistance in realizing their academic objectives." This entails activity in a number of areas: immigration advising, housing, orientation, financial aid, general advising and counseling, ombudsman work, liaison with institutional officials, liaison with sponsoring agencies, and some community-related work. Each of these areas is discussed further in Chapter Seven.

The manner in which work in these areas is approached varies, as we have already seen. In some smaller institutions, such as Alice's (see Chapter Two), FSA's do a great deal for foreign students, to the point of filling out immigration forms for them and making sure each one has a place to stay over the Christmas break.

At most other institutions, foreign students are expected to do more for themselves.

There seems to be no obvious place to draw the line between over-protectiveness (usually labelled "hand-holding") and laxity in deciding how much assistance to offer students. My own prejudice is that FSA's ought to see themselves as educators rather than surrogate parents, and ought to encourage foreign students to manage as well as they can on their own. In my view, students do not benefit from being trained to be dependent on an FSA or anyone else. But different people have different and quite respectable views on this question.

In addition to working in immigration, orientation, housing, and the other areas mentioned above, FSA's must assume leadership in the development of their institutions' overall policies and procedures concerning students from abroad. No one else is likely to do so. If an institution is to do a respectable job of attracting qualified foreign students and then treating them reasonably, the FSA will have to take the responsibility for reviewing policies and procedures, reporting any perceived deficiencies, and working with others to bring about improvement.

Culture learning.   To the minimal FSA job description just discussed, some people would add work in what John Walsh of the East-West Center calls "culture learning." This term refers to the idea of learning about culture and cultural differences in order to become more self-aware, more empathic, and better able to function in multicultural situations. At some institutions it is considered part of an FSA's responsibility to foster culture learning not only among foreign students and American students, but in the institution as a whole and among members of the community. My opinion is that work in the area of culture learning is inseparable from work in most of the minimal areas of FSA responsibility.

Activities aimed at culture learning take a variety of forms, including printed information, orientation programs, workshops on intercultural relations, professional development programs for staff and faculty, international festivals or fairs of various sorts, international houses and other such living arrangements, international student clubs, and some activities involving members of the community.

Chapter Seven contains further comments on work FSA's can do in the culture learning area.

Development.   Another area with which some FSA's are concerned, in addition to those falling within the minimal job description, is that of student responsibilities for economic development in their own countries. The basic idea here is that students who come to the United States from poorer countries can (and "should," in the view of many) use the education they receive in ways that will benefit their countries.

Work FSA's do in the development area might include recruiting students from poorer countries, finding financial aid for them, maintaining liaison with agencies that sponsor them, helping assure that their curricula are "relevant" to conditions in their own countries, and offering special programs or seminars on such topics as administration, teaching, communication, and social change.

NAFSA has long received U.S. Agency for International Development financial support for publications and programs aimed at AID-sponsored students. These AID-supported activities have fostered an interest in development-related issues among some foreign student advisers.

Globalism. A third area to which some FSA's devote attention bears various labels, including "globalism," "global education," "global awareness," and "awareness of interdependence." The general idea here is that the world's countries are involved with and mutually dependent upon each other, and the people of the United States are less than adequately prepared to participate in a world of interdependent peoples. Foreign students are seen as a vehicle for fostering a more global outlook. They are asked to serve as panelists, to make presentations and/or give interviews on such world issues as hunger, pollution, and human rights.

The globalism approach has probably suffered from lack of specificity in its concepts and objectives. "Globalism" and "awareness" are vague terms, not clear enough to serve as the basis for a well-planned educational program. A useful effort to make the idea clearer and more operational is Robert Hanvey's *An Attainable Global Perspective.*

So far in this chapter we have discussed varying conceptions of foreign students and the role of foreign student advisers. Continuing our consideration of some attitudes and ideas with which FSA's approach their responsibilities (however they conceive of those responsibilities), we turn our attention to the topic of the FSA's stance or posture *vis-a-vis* foreign students.

THE FSA'S STANCE VIS-A-VIS FOREIGN STUDENTS

Josef Mestenhauser once wrote an essay entitled "Are We Professionals, Semi-Professionals, or Dedicated Good Guys?" The way FSA's answer this question—whether or not they explicitly ask it of themselves—does much to determine how they will relate to their clients. The "professional" strives to keep personalities out of a case as much as possible, to be "objective" in determining facts and drawing conclusions, and then to make decisions based on standard practices or procedures. Judges, for example, are expected to disqualify themselves from considering cases in which they have a personal interest.

The "good guy," by contrast, wants to be liked and to do the nice or the good thing for others—at least for those others who are judged to deserve positive treatment.

The professional is likely to believe it is appropriate to maintain a measure of distance or detachment from clients. The good guy, on the other hand, is likely to favor (or at least permit) the development of personal friendships with clients.

There are advantages and disadvantages to both the professional and the good guy approaches. Some FSA's seem personally inclined to one and some to the other. The professional approach has the advantage of avoiding the appearance of favoritism and of making it easier for the FSA to say "no" to a student whose request presents problems. On the other hand, the professional approach forecloses the possibility of establishing personal relationships with many interesting people.

I have seen successful and effective FSA's of both the professional and the good guy types. My impression is that the FSA's personality, the FSA's role in the institution, and the institutional setting are the main determinants of an FSA's stance on this issue. Those with the professional approach are more likely to be found at larger institutions where the general administrative style tends to be more impersonal. The good guy approach is more likely to be encountered at smaller institutions.

Some professionals in the student affairs field adhere to what is called the "student development approach" to their work. This approach fosters a concern with helping students "develop" in ways that are deemed to represent advancements toward maturity and responsible adulthood. Katheryn Story, in an article in *College Student Personnel*, rightly points out that the theories on which the student development approach are based are products of U.S. cultural assumptions that do not apply to large numbers of foreign students. Story's main point is that the student development theories place a high value on individual autonomy and the achievement of self-reliance. Americans tend to assume that these are valuable traits. Many foreign students, and probably most people elsewhere in the world, have been taught to assume that maturity entails considerable concern for the well-being of others and for intra-group harmony. The "rugged individualists" that Americans admire are likely to be viewed as selfish and inconsiderate in many other societies. So "student development professionals" may need to modify their assumptions and approaches in order to work effectively with students from other countries.

The student development approach does have the advantage of calling attention to the fact that the people with whom student affairs personnel are working are whole people who are in a process of intellectual and social change, and not just bearers of isolated problems. For example, a foreign student who seeks financial aid is not just a person who needs money, but a person with some pride who might benefit from assistance with financial management, research into sources of financial support, and general decision-making. FSA's can serve their students more effectively if they are mindful of these broader aspects of the students' situations.

Another issue FSA's face concerns the degree to which it is appropriate to be "friends" with foreign students. This question can be particularly thorny for younger female FSA's. Many factors might impel foreign students and FSA's toward the development of close personal relationships. Are FSA's wise to encourage this, or even permit it? I would say not. FSA's run risks when they become friends, at least close ones, with their clients. They can lose their objectivity (to the degree that objectivity is possible in human relationships) and their credibility if they become closely affiliated with certain students. It becomes harder for them to apply professional standards in making decisions affecting those students. Other foreign students are more likely to see the FSA as one who plays favorites if the FSA is known to have (or thought to have) close friends among the students. Institutional colleagues are likely to develop doubts about an FSA's professional competence if the FSA's intimate friends include students from other countries. In other words, FSA's stand to lose influence among foreign students in general and among institutional colleagues if they are seen as having intimate relationships with certain students.

I believe FSA's are able to serve more students better in the long run if they make it a practice not to become involved in close personal relationships with people who are foreign students at their own institutions. Experience indicates that involvement in romantic relationships with foreign students is especially likely to damage an FSA's stature.

This is not to suggest that FSA's ought to be cold, aloof, or detached. Nor is it to suggest that FSA's will not have more of an affinity for some students than for others. FSA's can certainly be warm, cordial, and relatively open. They are likely to find that some particular students are drawn to them personally and to the kind of work the FSA's office is doing. That does not necessarily cause difficulties. Difficulties ensue from intimate relationships with particular students, especially those who are members of the opposite sex.

I am inclined to believe that it is unwise for *any* full-time employee of a foreign student office to become intimate friends with clients of the office.

PROBLEM OWNERSHIP

"Problem ownership" refers to one's notion of the locus of responsibility for a problem. To "own a problem" is to be in a situation in which one's needs are not being met, or where one is dissatisfied with one's own behavior (Thomas Gordon discusses this concept in all of his "effectiveness training" books). FSA's, like everyone else, can save themselves considerable psychological stress and clarify possible courses of action by paying close attention, when presented with a problem, to the question of whose problem it is. Many people, including some who are attracted to foreign student advising because it offers a chance to help others, cause difficulty for themselves and others by failing to consider the question of problem ownership.

Take, for example, the not uncommon situation of the newly arrived foreign student who tells the FSA that he does not have enough money to enroll and that he needs financial aid. Whose problem is this? Many FSA's assume it is theirs, because the student who has the problem is foreign. Certainly the student can be expected to try to induce the FSA to buy into the problem. But who caused the problem? The student did, unless the institution understated the amount of money the student would need, something institutions rarely do. Who suffers if the problem is not solved? The student does. Who owns this problem? The student does. Should the FSA take action on this student's behalf? We will consider that question in a moment.

Applications

The concept of problem ownership has three important applications in foreign student advising: as a tool for economizing effort, an aid in maintaining mental health, and as a device for helping students gain perspective.

Economizing effort. FSA's (unless they are lacking influence) generally have more than enough work to do. This means that they must choose from among many possible activities. In making those choices, problem ownership is an important criterion to consider. Should the FSA in the previous example take time to seek money for the student who arrived short of funds? Probably not, unless there is not enough other work to do. The FSA might suggest that the student find a less expensive school or postpone registration, but the FSA would be unwise to enter the time-consuming effort of raising money to solve this student's self-made problem. Time and anguish saved by clarifying the ownership of a problem enables FSA's to better provide their services to foreign students in general.

Helping maintain an FSA's mental health. There are too many problems in the world—and even on any particular American campus—for one individual to solve. People who take all the world's problems as their own are likely to lack adequate insight into that fact. They work for awhile on this problem and for awhile on that and they worry about all that is left to be done. They are thereby rendered exhausted and distracted, unable to work consistently and effectively on those problems they are actually in a position to do something about. People in the so-called "helping professions" are particularly susceptible to this malady, because they sympathize with troubled people and want to help them.

An effective FSA needs a clear mind and an adequate supply of mental and physical energy. Effective FSA's know they cannot resolve all the problems students bring them as a result of such things as civil wars in the Middle East, currency devaluations in Latin America, deaths in families in Hong Kong, Professor X's unfair grading system, or a student's failure to employ a reliable method of birth control. Effective FSA's know that unfortunate things happen to people and that some of those unfortunate things will require their victims to make radical changes in their plans. Some foreign students might, for example, have to delay graduation, take a job they would prefer not to take, ask a cousin for a loan, or even abandon, at least temporarily, their academic objectives.

FSA's are in a position where they can cripple themselves by worrying about and working on problems they do not own and cannot remedy. They will be mentally healthier, and therefore more capable of being effective, if they take care to determine which of the problems they encounter are their own and which they are in a position to do something about.

Helping students gain perspective. Like FSA's, foreign students (and nearly everyone else) can gain perspective on their own circumstances and thereby improve their own mental health if they incorporate the notion of problem ownership into their outlooks. FSA's may have opportunities, in the course of their advising and counseling, to help students do so. One student came to me very upset because a group of his compatriots were making fools of themselves, he said, by parading in front of a principal campus building every day in the name of a certain political cause. Not only were they making fools of themselves, he said, but they were conveying an embarrassing image of people from his country. This was disturbing him to the point where he was not sleeping well or studying effectively.

I offered this student an explanation of the problem ownership idea. I then asked him to explain to me how the problem he presented could be considered his problem. He could not do so, of course, because the problem was not his. If his compatriots wanted to make fools of themselves, that was their business. If the natives were unwise enough to generalize too much from the demontrators' example, that was their problem. The student saw that, and went away, he said, relieved of a large burden.

Many students' problems essentially vanish when the students learn to distinguish between their own and others' problems, and to realize how pointless it is to expend their mental energy on problems they did not create, are not really victims of, or cannot remedy.

For more discussion of the problem ownership idea, and examples drawn from administrative situations, see Thomas Gordon's *Leader Effectiveness Training.*

The final topic of this chapter, professional standards, is a more general one than that of problem ownership. The idea of problem ownership can be clearly and specifically put into operation on a daily basis. Professional standards in foreign student advising are more nebulous.

PROFESSIONAL STANDARDS

Like many other national associations, the National Association for Foreign Student Affairs (NAFSA) has recently felt compelled to give concerted attention to the topic of standards or ethical guidelines. The question of standards in foreign student affairs gained national attention not long ago when it became known that some educational institutions were essentially selling admission to foreign applicants who, it was thought, could contribute needed tuition income.

Like many other national associations, NAFSA has struggled with the topic of standards. When a large organization encompassing diverse interests tries to agree on something as important as standards of performance, some intractable issues arise: Who is to decide what the published standards are to be? What enforcement mechanisms, if any, should be established? How will violators be punished?

NAFSA continues to work toward answers to these difficult questions. Its Board of Directors has chosen the self-study and self-regulation approach, and the organization is developing self-study procedures and guidelines for its members.

Meanwhile, two NAFSA publications in this area are worthy of note, not because they are entirely clear and specific but because they represent the closest thing to concensus the only "professional association" in educational interchange has been able to achieve. *Standards and Responsibilities in International Educational Interchange* is a 21-page booklet that all FSA's are advised to own, be familiar with, and share with institutional colleagues who are interested in foreign students. NAFSA's address, along with those of other educational organizations mentioned in this *Handbook*, is given in Appendix F.

A shorter statement of standards, "NAFSA Principles for International Educational Exchange," is reproduced in Appendix G.

FSA's may feel frustrated by the vagueness of the NAFSA publications about professional standards. The publications provide guidance only at a fairly general level. They say, for example, that an institution admitting foreign students has an obligation to provide supplementary services those students need, but they do not say how many FSA's ought to be on the staff, or what their job descriptions ought to contain. Again we encounter the fact that FSA's, when faced with questions about the proper way to proceed, are often left almost entirely to decide for themselves.

☞ 5

Knowledge

THERE ARE MANY things a foreign student adviser can benefit from knowing. An FSA's store of knowledge is called upon to aid in understanding and explaining to different audiences a remarkably diverse array of situations. This chapter discusses knowledge with which FSA's will want to be familiar.

Knowledgeability was among the variables listed in Chapter Two as affecting a person's influence. The more FSA's know about the topics discussed in this chapter, the more influence they are likely to have. In this chapter, knowledge that is useful to FSA's is rather arbitrarily divided into the following categories: self, institution, community, professional colleagues, external agencies, clients' backgrounds, applied linguistics, current affairs, intercultural communication, and immigration regulations.

SELF-KNOWLEDGE

We have already (in Chapter Three) discussed self-awareness as a valuable characteristic for FSA's. That, of course, is an aspect of self-knowledge. The two terms can be distinguished by saying that self-awareness pertains to a moment-by-moment consciousness of what is happening within oneself and with respect to others in a given situation. Self-knowledge is a more inclusive notion, referring to a general familiarity with one's own enduring characteristics and proclivities. For our purposes, the important aspects of self are strengths and weaknesses, values, and "buttons."

Strengths and weaknesses

It is helpful for FSA's to know what they do well (remember detailed matters such as immigration regulations, for example, or stay calm under pressure) and what they do poorly (writing reports, meeting deadlines, etc.). Then they can delegate to others those necessary tasks they know they cannot do well, or work to improve in their areas of weakness, or both.

Values

As used here, "values" refers to preferences and to convictions about what is right and what is wrong. Different people have different sets of values, of course, and it helps us to know our own and to have an idea how ours compare with those of others. I find it helpful to remind myself, for example, that I place a higher value than many other people on verbal articulateness. Many others rank sociability higher than I do. By being aware of my own values (as best I can), I can better understand my own reactions to other people and theirs to me.

"Buttons"

"Buttons" is not a scientific term, but it conveys nicely the common sense notion that we all have certain kinds of events, topics, situations, or people that "set us off" on some seemingly predetermined and automatic response. When our buttons are pushed, we are not usually able to be attentive to others, as self-aware as we might otherwise be, or as able to behave in rational or constructive ways. Buttons that commonly get pushed in foreign student advising work include those related to sexism, perceived dishonesty, perceived "pushiness," prejudice among the natives, and foreign students who want to immigrate.

Good FSA's know what their buttons are. They work consciously to reduce the number and the sensitivity of their buttons. And they try, when they realize that one of their buttons has been pushed, to stop talking, to regain control, and to request help if that seems advisable.

INSTITUTION

FSA's work in organizations, of course. To get things accomplished, they must be able to work constructively within those organizations. That requires knowing their institutions' missions, procedures, and personnel.

Missions

Different educational institutions have different overall objectives or missions. Small, private colleges do not have the same missions as large, research-oriented universities. FSA's had better know the *raison-d-etre* of their own institutions, so they can behave accordingly, make plans or design programs that are in harmony with the institution's overall direction, and help foreign students understand (which they often do not, at least at first) what sort of institution they are attending.

FSA's will want to be mindful of the possibility that there may be discrepancies between their institutions' stated missions and the objectives that are actually being sought. And they will also want to realize that an institution's mission might somehow be or become incompatible with their own values or interests, making it seem appropriate for them to seek employment elsewhere.

Procedures

Even small educational institutions in the United States are likely to have detailed procedures for many matters that concern students. Examples are legion: gaining admission, proficiency testing, paying tuition, checking out library books, registering for classes, registering automobiles, getting health insurance, and on, and on. The more FSA's know about these procedures, or at least where to get information about them, the better they will be able to aid their foreign student clients. They will certainly want to have on hand the institution's catalogue, student handbook, and any publications containing formal rules and procedures.

Personnel

It is not mission statements or procedure manuals that make institutions operate, but the people who work in them. FSA's will want to know the personnel of their institutions on both the formal and informal levels.

Formal. Institutions differ strikingly in the degree to which they stress formality in day-to-day operations. At some institutions, nearly everything is written down and the written words are followed. At others more is done informally, whether or not much is written down. However much stress is placed on formality within their institutions, FSA's will want to know the organization chart. Who reports to whom? What procedures are carried out and what decisions are made in which offices?

One aspect of formal organization that rarely appears on educational institution's organization charts is that of committees. Effective FSA's know what institutional committees have or might take an interest in foreign student affairs. Furthermore, they know what those committees are formally charged to accomplish, who the members are, and what role the committees actually play in institutional governance. It may turn out, for example, that a particular committee, despite its promising charge and composition, is ineffective in practice, and could not help an FSA bring about some desirable change in institutional policy or procedure.

Informal. It is important for FSA's to know not just the formal institutional structure, but the individuals who occupy the positions listed on the chart. The ideal is to have a cordial personal relationship with as many institutional colleagues as possible, since FSA's may have occasion to interact with personnel in all parts of the institution. Appendix H lists institutional personnel an FSA might benfit from knowing. The personal characteristic of sociability, discussed in Chapter Three, may be more important here than in any other aspect of the FSA's work.

I have repeatedly been struck, in my work as a consultant, by the number of instances in which FSA's do not have cordial relationships with their institutional colleagues. Sometimes they have acrimonious relationships; more often they simply do not know many of their colleagues and have not taken the trouble to become acquainted. Often the FSA's and their colleagues have built up images of each other, and have come to think they know each other's viewpoints and values. They operate (inevitably) on the basis of their images or perceptions of each other. When consultants visit and talk with all parties, it becomes clear that the perceptions are mutually inaccurate. (Usually the people are more in agreement with each other than they realize.)

There is considerable irony in these situations. We find people who, in their role as FSA's, are trying to devise ways to encourage constructive interaction between foreign students and their hosts, with the object of breaking down stereotypes and developing mutual understanding and respect among real human beings. At the same time, the FSA's are not interacting constructively with their own institutional colleagues, and are building rather than breaking down stereotypes and false assumptions about them.

When FSA's urge interaction between foreign students and their hosts, with the intention of building constructive relationships based on knowledge and respect, they need to make sure they are putting their own advice into practice.

Becoming acquainted with institutional colleagues has at least two salutary outcomes. One is more obvious than the other, but both are important. First, FSA's and colleagues who know each other can see each other as individuals rather than as members of groups about which they hold misleading stereotypes.

Second, becoming personally acquainted with each other helps institutional colleagues learn about each other's *situations*. Brislin offers some extremely interesting ideas about the role of situations in human conduct. Those ideas would be relevant in many parts of this *Handbook*. They are summarized here.

Brislin says that people normally look for some motivation behind other people's behavior. Generally, they attribute the behavior either to some *trait* of the other person as an individual or to the *situation* in which the individual is operating. He says that situations explain more about people's behavior than is generally realized. In cases where we are familiar with other people's situations we tend, rightly, to attribute much of what they do to the situations they are in rather than to their individual traits. If we are not familiar with their situations, we are likely to commit what is called the "fundamental attribution error," ascribing their behavior to their traits rather than to their situations.

Brislin is writing about intercultural situations. He makes the point that people in cross-cultural encounters are unlikely to be familiar with each other's situations and so are prone to make the fundamental attribution error. That error will also be made among institutional colleagues who have not come to know each other's individual characteristics *and* situations.

FSA's who know their colleagues' situations will have a number of advantages. They will be able to understand their colleagues' behavior better; they will more likely be able to empathize with them and thus build influence with them; and they will be able to serve their foreign student clients better by providing more accurate explanations of the behavior of particular faculty and staff members.

Those aspects of their colleagues' situations that FSA's might want to learn about include their job descriptions, their workloads, the political situations within their offices, the values and operating methods of their supervisors, and personal issues they may be confronting. All these (and no doubt many other) aspects of colleagues' situations will shape their behavior, apart from any of their personal traits.

It is not the intention here to suggest that FSA's, if they should make the effort, will always have harmonious relationships with institutional colleagues. They probably will not. Value conflicts and personality clashes seem inevitable. The suggestion here is to strive to maintain a minimal level of civility and politeness even in the face of the strongest of conflicts. Displays of temper, vindictive actions, and principled refusals to interact may provide momentary pleasure, but in the longer term rarely have the beneficial results of patience and politeness.

A final suggestion concerning the informal aspect of knowing one's institution: Take the trouble to know and be respectful of secretaries. It is as common to hear that advice being offered as it is to see it being ignored. Secretaries are essential to the operation of any organization. Secretaries in educational institutions sometimes offer students important social support and advice. They can often help FSA's get needed information, or remedy students' problems. Being in good stead with secretaries can enhance an FSA's influence in the institution.

COMMUNITY

Whether or not they are actively involved in host family organizations or other community programs of the kinds discussed in Chapter Seven, FSA's will want to know a number of people in the community and be familiar with certain community organizations. These include civic officials, civic leaders, media representatives, helping agencies, service organizations, and what I will call generous, helpful individuals.

Civic officials

It is advisable for an FSA to know, at a minimum, appropriate government officials and law enforcement officers. In a small town this might mean knowing the mayor and the chief of police; in a large city it might mean knowing city council members and the head of the nearest police station. Ideally, these civic officials will know who the FSA is, what general responsibilities the FSA has, and what situations can usefully be brought to the FSA's attention.

Civic leaders

FSA's can sometimes get help of assorted kinds if they are acquainted with the community's influential citizens. Those citizens might aid in circumstances that require emergency assistance of some kind, sustained fund raising, favorable public relations, or just a word from an influential person.

Media representatives

International educational interchange, like so much else in contemporary U.S. society, can be dramatically helped or harmed by the media. If they know local media representatives, FSA's can sometimes help cast a positive light on some aspect of educational exchange, or at least help provide a balanced view of a situation in which only the negative side is gaining attention.

Helping agencies

Foreign students sometimes get into situations where they could benefit from the services of various helping agencies that can be found in many communities. Such agencies offer help in a variety of areas, including legal aid, financial counseling, spouse abuse and other family counseling, alcoholism prevention, education for gifted children, and opportunities for voluntary service. FSA's will want to know what organizations of this type have services that are available to students from other countries.

Service organizations

Service organizations such as Rotary, Kiwanis, and Lions clubs sometimes have international interests. These interests might involve fund raising, sponsoring trips or other educational or social programs, or helping recruit host families. Some church groups will support projects of these kinds. FSA's enlarge their ability to serve their students if they know about the service organizations in their communities. Directories of these and other kinds of community organizations are often available from chambers of commerce.

Generous, helpful individuals

In most communities there are people who are willing to give help to others who need it. They might provide temporary housing, transportation for some excursion, help in locating apartments, English conversation practice, used furniture, or whatever. In many communities these individuals have created relatively formal organizations whose objectives include providing such services to people from abroad, and promoting culture learning as well. FSA's will want to know as many of these people as possible, work closely with the organizations they may have established, and be certain they receive appropriate recognition for their efforts and contributions.

PROFESSIONAL COLLEAGUES

Sometimes foreign student advisers at other institutions are an FSA's best source of information, advice, and moral support. (Some FSA's work at institutions where "no one else understands.") At a minimum, an FSA will want to know (1) the FSA in the same INS district who is the best informed about immigration regulations, (2) an FSA anywhere who is well informed about immigration regulations, and (3) at least one experienced FSA at an institution of the same general size and type as one's own.

Meeting fellow FSA's most commonly takes place at NAFSA conferences and workshops. Going to visit them in their offices is another approach. In the absence of these possibilities, a relationship can be developed over the phone. FSA's in general are well known for their willingness to assist colleagues at other institutions.

Foreign admissions officers, teachers of English as a second language, and others involved in educational exchange can also provide FSA's with information and support.

EXTERNAL AGENCIES

The term "external agencies" refers here to two different kinds of organizations. The first is U.S. government agencies whose activities affect foreign students. The principal one, of course, is the Immigration and Naturalization Service, about which more will be said later in this chapter. Other federal agencies whose work touches on the interests of at least some FSA's are the Visa Office of the Department of State, the Exchange-Visitor Programs Branch of the Bureau of Educational and Cultural Affairs in the U.S. Information Agency, the Manpower Administration branch of the Department of Labor, the U.S. Agency for International Development, and the Social Security Administration.

The second kind of organization is that which sponsors or at least oversees foreign students in the United States. This includes both non-profit educational agencies (such as the Institute of International Education, the African-American Institute, the Latin American Scholarship Program of American Universities, and the American-Mideast Educational and Training Service) and certain foreign governments whose representatives at embassies, consulates, or special offices in the United States administer scholarship programs here. Examples (at this writing) include Nigeria, Malaysia, and Saudi Arabia.

Not all FSA's have occasion to deal with all these agencies. They all deal with the INS, of course, but their need to be familiar with the other agencies depends on where their foreign students come from, what sponsorship arrangements they have, and what immigration status they hold.

FSA's can serve their students better, and thus increase their own influence, if they are familiar with the following aspects of those external agencies with which they have occasion to interact:

1. the agency's mission

2. its procedures affecting students at the FSA's institution

3. the personnel responsible for those procedures

With respect to the personnel of external agencies, it is well to know not just the formal structure but also the informal centers of responsibility and lines of communication, and not just the individuals but also their situations. (Compare the discussion above about knowing personnel at one's own institution.) One cannot hope to fathom the workings of the INS or the Nigerian Embassy or consulates, for example, without some knowledge of the situations of the people who work there.

There are many ways of learning about external agencies. Some of the agencies publish descriptive brochures or annual reports that

give an official view. Some send representatives to NAFSA conferences, or will do so if invited. Some send representatives to visit
campuses. Telephone conversations with staff members can be
revealing; conversations with ex-staff members even more so. FSA's
at other institutions can often provide useful information. Foreign
students themselves sometimes know how their embassies, consulates, or sponsoring agencies operate. Sometimes they think they
know and they do not, because they have believed a rumor or
overgeneralized from a particular experience.

Most FSA's use all these means of learning about the external
agencies with which they deal.

CLIENTS' BACKGROUNDS

FSA's and their foreign student clients benefit in several ways
when FSA's have some knowledge of the students' educational and
cultural backgrounds. First, the FSA's can better understand the
new situation the students are in and the particular adjustments and
accommodations they will have to make.

Second, FSA's can more effectively explain things to new students
if they are able to use examples and comparisons that relate to the
students' own experiences. FSA's add to their influence with students when the students can see that FSA's know something about
their respective educational systems and cultural backgrounds.

Third, FSA's can more effectively serve as intermediaries
between foreign students, on the one hand, and institutional faculty
and staff, on the other, if they are familiar with the students'
backgrounds.

At institutions with a small number of students from other countries, FSA's might be able to learn not just about the students' general educational and cultural backgrounds, but about each student's
particular experiences and aspirations.

Let us look in a little detail at the kinds of information it is useful
for FSA's to have about their students' educational and cultural
backgrounds.

Educational backgrounds

Most of what FSA's will want to know about the educational
systems in their clients' countries is classified under the headings of
sociology of education and comparative education. FSA's who do
admissions work will need to verse themselves in these areas. Here is

a set of questions FSA's might ask about each educational system they wish to understand:

1. What is the official ideal concerning education for the country's citizens? (Until recently, at least, the official ideal in the United States has been that as many people as possible should get as much formal education as possible. Other official ideals might be less expansive, limiting higher education to a smaller portion of the population.)

2. What is the nature of the national government's role in education? (More specifically, what is the government's role in setting curriculum? Standards? Is the government using the educational system in some deliberate way to accomplish any special social or political goal, such as imposition of a national language or the encouragement of diverse ethnic identities?)

3. From what social strata and geographic areas do most students come?

4. What entrance and leaving examinations are required at each level? What portion of those who attempt the examinations pass them?

5. What curricula are normally followed by college-bound pupils?

6. What changes and controversies (there usually are some) are currently engaging the attention of people in the field of education?

7. What methods of education (lecture, laboratory, problem-solving, etc.) predominate?

8. What is the predominant conception of the nature of education? (In the United States, the predominant conception, particularly at the post-secondary level and beyond, is that of a continuously expanding body of knowledge being accumulated and reexamined by scholars and by students as well. A contrasting conception, to be found in much of the Middle East, is that of a fixed body of knowledge and wisdom being transmitted from teachers to students.)

9. What intellectual skills (for example, memorization, in-depth analysis, synthesis) does the system reward?

10. How is students' academic work evaluated?

Some knowledge of the responses to each of these questions will make FSA's reasonably well-informed about the educational systems of their students' countries.

Whatever their educational backgrounds, most foreign students in the United States find certain aspects of the American system of higher education novel. The aspects to which they are most likely to have to make some adjustments are the following:

1. having to select from among a number of possible courses rather than following a completely prescribed curriculum

2. being assigned an academic adviser rather than simply reading about courses that must be taken

3. specializing later rather than earlier in the undergraduate program and thus having to take courses outside one's area of interest in order to obtain a "liberal education"

4. having to take objective-type tests (such as true-false and multiple choice) rather than, or in addition to, subjective-type (essay) examinations

5. dealing with a sometimes complex system for registering for classes each term

6. having relatively frequent assignments and examinations or quizzes rather than being left to work more independently and at a leisurely pace

7. encountering classmates, especially at the freshman and sophomore levels, who seem ill-prepared for post-secondary work and not very highly motivated to succeed at it

8. being expected to raise questions and participate in class discussions rather than sitting quietly and accepting the teacher's word on all matters

9. encountering competitiveness among students, especially in professional or graduate level classes

10. having to analyze and synthesize the material to which they are exposed, especially at the graduate level

11. being expected to use the library extensively

12. having a great deal of importance attached to grades

13. having to do what they might consider menial tasks in laboratory courses

14. being liable to punishment for activities deemed to constitute "cheating" or plagiarism

FSA's will want to know about these characteristics of American post-secondary education so they can understand students' reactions to them and help the students adjust to the demands and expectations of the system.

Cultural backgrounds

The topic of foreign students' cultural backgrounds is exceedingly complex. Anthropologists, who have the longest record of "scientific" interest in culture and cultural differences, have not reached an agreement as to how the topic is best approached. Nor have social psychologists, some of whom have more recently become interested in the phenomena of culture, culture contact, and adjustment to new cultures. We will elaborate a bit on some of these issues later in this chapter, under the heading of "intercultural communication." Meanwhile, we will offer another list of questions, ones FSA's might want to ask about their students' cultural backgrounds. These questions relate to situations that include students, faculty and staff, and bureaucracies. Many more questions could be asked; these are but a few:

1. How are differences in status (for example, student-teacher) handled?

2. What is the prevalent conception of the locus of control over people's lives? (That is, are the things that happen to people usually viewed as products of their own behavior, of the workings of political or social forces, of "fate," or of some other factor?)

3. What are the predominant friendship patterns (with respect to length of relationship and extent of mutual obligation)?

4. What are the most common forms of verbal interaction in everyday relations (with respect to the following: discussion topics that are considered appropriate in various situations, volume of voice, length of each separate contribution to a conversation, style of interaction [debate, argument, ritual exchange], and nonverbal accompaniments to speech)?

5. Where (if anywhere) do people go for help with personal problems?

6. What assumptions shape male-female relationships?

7. What kinds of evidence (scientific tests, personal observations, the word of the Prophet, etc.) are considered persuasive?

The answers to these and related questions will help an FSA begin to know another culture.

Sources of information about the educational and cultural backgrounds of foreign students

Some people spend their entire professional lives studying selected aspects of the cultures and educational systems of just one or perhaps a few other countries. FSA's clearly cannot do that. They must content themselves with general familiarity with their students' backgrounds. Publications, professional colleagues, and foreign students themselves can provide them useful information.

Publications. There are disappointingly few publications whose specific purpose is to acquaint educational exchange personnel with the educational and cultural backgrounds of specific groups of foreign students. Two such publications are Orin Parker's *Cultural Clues to the Middle Eastern Student* and my own *Students from the Arab World and Iran.* Both NAFSA and AACRAO (American Association of Collegiate Registrars and Admissions Officers, address in Appendix F) have publications concerning the educational systems of various countries. A list of these and related publications is available from NAFSA in the form of an "ADSEC Bibliography."

There Is a Difference: 17 Intercultural Perspecirves, by John Fieg and John Blair, offers short chapters on the perspectives of visitorsfrom seventeen different countries, as well as a chapter on American values.

NAFSA's Community Section has compiled what is called the "COMSEC Bibliography" of anthropological studies, travelers' accounts, and novels concerning many countries. A wise FSA will get this bibliography and use it extensively.

Of course, library card catalogues and guides to periodicals can lead readers to countless other publications about foreign educational systems and cultures.

Professional colleagues. It is the job of foreign admissions specialists to know or have ready access to information about foreign educational systems. FSA's can borrow these materials from the admissions personnel on their campuses.

Many faculty members are knowledgeable about at least some apsects of other countries as a result of their academic studies and/or having been born or lived abroad. Certainly they can be called upon to help FSA's learn about foreign students' backgrounds. Both NAFSA and AACRAO have their acknowledged experts on specific foreign countries, and these individuals are normally pleased to respond to inquiries.

Foreign students. Foreign students can teach FSA's much that they would benefit from knowing about other countries. The two sets of questions presented earlier in this section, when addressed to foreign students, will generate many interesting ideas. (The questions on the cultural background list are most likely to be understood and answered appropriately if they are prefaced by the phrase, "Compared to what you have seen in the United States, . . .")

I like to organize sessions in which a panel of students (selected for dispassion and articulateness in English) from a particular country or world area address a set of questions before an audience of faculty and staff who have occasion to interact with students from that country or area. The questions, presented in Appendix I, concern the educational system and cultural background of their county or area as compared to the United States. Holding a session of this kind serves a number of beneficial purposes. It helps FSA's and other institutional personnel gain useful information; it promotes constructive relationships and attitudes between foreign students and the faculty and staff who attend; it contributes to the realization that foreign students can make valuable contributions to the institution; and it gives the foreign students the pleasurable experience of being in the role of expert, an experience for which the FSA is seen to be responsible. All of these beneficial outcomes strengthen the FSA's influence among students, staff, and faculty.

The issues facing foreign students

Foreigners anywhere face certain issues or problems.[1] Of course, the nature and severity of those problems vary. The variations seem

---

[1] *A Community in Limbo* (Nash, 1970) is a very provocative anthropological study of the American community in a city in Spain. It is based on interviews and the study of some documents. Nash offers a typology of adjustment styles: bohemian, creative, and philistine. Among the variables he thinks affect the foreigners' reactions are their social status; organizational affiliations; past experiences in other cultures (especially whether or not they have experience in a less rationally-oriented culture); sex; personality type (organization man vs. individualist); amount of support from the home organization; relations with other Americans in the community; and relations with hosts.

One can think in comparable terms about foreign students in the United States and come up with some interesting ideas.

to depend on the individual characteristics and the cultural backgrounds of the people involved and on the situations in which the foreigners find themselves. Much research suggests, for example, that African and Asian students in the United States have more serious adjustment difficulties than do students from Europe and Oceania. (Lee, Abd-Ella, & Burks, 1981) This is presumably because the cultural difference are somehow greater. Many writers (e.g., Kohls, 1979, and Hammar, Gudykunst, & Wiseman, 1978) have sought to list the personality characteristics that correlate with good adjustment to intercultural situations.

Because there is so much variation in the nature and severity of problems foreign students in the United States encounter, one must be cautious in generalizing about them. But FSA's will want to have some broad perspectives on these problems. A few generalizations are therefore offered here. FSA's can refine these generalizations by measuring them against the characteristics of the foreign students at their own institutions. The students' English proficiency, fields and level of study, cultural backgrounds, and general level of sophistication all influence the nature of their reactions to their new settings.

To some degree, most foreign students can be expected to face a number of transitory problems. The obvious ones are adjusting to new food, climate, and types of housing. New students may painfully miss family and friends. They are unlikely to have friends in the new setting, a fact that has an especially adverse effect on some students.

Some foreign students suffer from "status shock" when they come to the United States. Those who have been out of school and employed and those who come from one of the many countries where post-secondary students are accorded a noticeable amount of social status or respect are often disturbed to find that in the United States the status of college and university students is relatively low.

Whether or not they suffer from status shock, most new foreign students will experience the discomfort of being treated as stereotypes rather than as individuals. The natives will treat them as "foreign students" or perhaps "Orientals" (or "Latins," or "Arabs," etc.) rather than as the individuals whom people at home have known them to be. This experience is often perceived as demeaning.

Most new foreign students, whatever their English proficiency level, need some time to adjust to local English. Regional accents, contemporary slang, and the local pace of speaking will be new. Some students make these adjustments within a few days; others require weeks or months. It is not at all unusual for new students to be surprised and even depressed when they discover that they cannot readily understand the local people and that the local people have trouble understanding them.

Beyond these usually transitory problems facing foreign students are some more enduring sources of stress. Persistent financial shortages afflict many students, sometimes because they have planned poorly and sometimes because events beyond their control have reduced their income and/or increased their expenses.

Prejudice or at least condescension from the natives bother most foreign students throughout their stays in the United States. (See Chapter Four, the section on "Conceptions of Foreign Students.") So do the Amercans' low level of knowledge of and interest in other countries, and the paucity of sophisticated international reporting in the U.S. media.

Finally, unwelcome events in their own countries can cause continuing problems for foreign students in the United States. Events which endanger lives or property, damage their families' financial situations, or endanger their prospects for rewarding employment at home all cause preoccupation among students from abroad.

The foregoing catalogue risks leaving the impression that foreign students are continuously plagued by problems. That impression would be misleading. It is not at all unusual to encounter foreign students who view their assorted "problems" as interesting challenges and who cheerfully learn from the new situations they encounter.

APPLIED LINGUISTICS

Knowing something about applied linguistics, and especially about the specialized topic of teaching English as a foreign language (TEFL), helps FSA's understand the language problems many of their clients face. FSA's will want to be familiar with the problems encountered by both English learners and TEFL teachers. It is important also to have a good understanding of the TOEFL (Test of English as a Foreign Language)—what it seeks to measure, how it is structured, what its scores mean, and what its limitations are. FSA's have frequent occasion to explain the significance of

TOEFL scores to faculty members. Some institutions use scores from two other English proficiency examinations, the ALIGU (from the American Language Institute of Georgetown University) and the Michigan Test (from the University of Michigan's Langugage Institute).

Skimming TEFL texts at various levels of proficiency and talking with TEFL teachers are probably the best ways for FSA's to learn about relevant aspects of applied linguistics. It is especially instructive to hear TEFL teachers discuss the particular English-learning problems of speakers of particular other languages.

The Educational Testing Service publication *TOEFL Test and Score Manual* gives a comprehensive description of the TOEFL. See Appendix F for the address.

CURRENT AFFAIRS

Foreign students are sometimes dramatically affected by political and economic events occurring in their own countries or among various countries. FSA's will want to have at least some basic understanding of the political systems and contemporary issues in their students' countries. It helps to know these things:

1. What is the basic political system?
2. What is the basic economic system?
3. What internal issues does the country currently face?
4. What intergroup (ethnic, linguistic, religious) differences exist and how salient are they? (These differences often carry over into the relationships among students from a particular country when they come to the United States.)
5. How likely is the country to experience a major disruption of some type (e.g., civil war, radical change of governments, drastic currency devaluation, armed international conflict)?

To have some context for understanding these questions and their answers, FSA's might want to read one or two introductory texts in political science, international politics, and international economics. They will find it helpful to keep informed about developments in their students' countries or at least to bring themselves up-to-date quickly should some drastic event occur. Many FSA's consider the *Christian Science Monitor* to be a particularly good source of information about international affairs.

In some previous sections of this chapter I have suggested getting information from students themselves about aspects of their own countries. But I would urge caution in discussing politics with foreign students. I have come to believe that many foreign students harbor doubts about foreign student advisers' intentions and allegiances. Many foreign students, it appears to me, believe or suspect that FSA's are somehow in the intelligence gathering business. This impression gets strong support when an FSA begins to ask questions about the domestic politics of a student's country, especially if the questions might lead to a revelation of the student's own political opinions or affiliations. Other FSA's have different views on this matter; for my part, I rarely introduce political questions into a conversation with a foreign student I do not know reasonably well, and I try assiduously to avoid any questioning that might be construed as an effort to get a student to divulge personal political views. Discussions about general political or social issues, as opposed to ones about a student's own views, are quite acceptable. Many students enjoy talking about politics, and it is a compliment to them when an FSA manifests some knowledge of political and social issues that are pertinent in their countries.

It is not just international politics about which FSA's will want to stay informed, but national and state politics as well. Congressional actions affecting immigration law and appropriations for activities related to international education concern foreign students and therefore FSA's. FSA's ought not only to stay informed on these matters, but ought to express their opinions to legislators and administrative officials and be ready to mobilize institutional representatives in support of national policy that favors international educational interchange.

FSA's in state-supported institutions will want to be informed about proposed state government measures that would affect foreign students. Many such measures have been advanced in the past few years and most of them would have had a detrimental impact on foreign student programs. They included special, higher tuition rates for foreign students, and assorted restrictions on their enrollment.

INTERCULTURAL COMMUNICATION

Over the past 15 years or so, the topic of "intercultural communication" has attracted more and more attention from scholars in diverse disciplines and from practitioners in international education. If we define "intercultural communication" as communication between people from different cultures, we can immediately see that it is central to the daily work of foreign student advisers. All of the following FSA activities involve intercultural communication: preparing written information for foreign students; advising, counseling, and all other daily interactions with students from abroad; serving as an intermediary or "cultural interpreter" between foreign students and others; designing and conducting educational programs intended to improve intercultural relationships; and working with foreign student and community organizations (see my essay, "Intercultural Communication Central to Educational Exchange").

FSA's will want to learn as much as they can about intercultural communication, because it will help them do their jobs better. In general, what FSA's will want to learn from the intercultural communication field comes under three headings: comparing cultures, describing reactions to the encounter with new cultures, and prescribing conduct for improved intercultural relations.

Comparing cultures

We can easily see that, in general, Nigerians do not behave in the same way as Japanese. Their cultural backgrounds make a difference. But how can those differences be conceptualized and described? What are the differences (and similarities) between Nigerians and Japanese or between other combinations of cultural groups? How can we discuss these differences when we are talking with foreign students and others? While no agreed-upon framework for comparing cultures has emerged from the work of scholars, three avenues of study have produced some useful ideas. They are comparisons of (1) assumptions and values, (2) patterns of thought, and (3) communicative styles.

Assumptions and values. Starting from the work of the Kluckhohns, several scholars have sought to elucidate the idea that people growing up in different cultures are taught different assumptions and values about the nature of man, interpersonal relationships, man-nature relationships, and relationships between man and the supernatural. Stephen Rhinesmith applies this framework to interpersonal relationships between people of different cultures. Edward Stewart uses it to compare "American" to other cultures.

John Condon & Fathi Yousef present an elaborate typology for comparing what they call "value orientations" of different cultures. These ideas can help FSA's understand how some of their clients' basic ideas compare with those of Americans.

Patterns of thought. It seems to be the case that cultures differ with respect to the way their members reach conclusions in their thought and arguments. Different people give differing amounts of weight to different forms of evidence. What is "logical" in one place may be illogical, nonsensical, or irrelevant elsewhere. Condon & Yousef have an interesting chapter on this subject. Michael Cole & Sylvia Means discuss it at greater length. Of course, this topic is of special interest to foreign students (and thus to FSA's) because they need to learn to use the natives' patterns of thought in order to achieve academic success here.

Communicative style. Dean Barnlund, in his study of Japanese and American self-concepts, develops the idea that people from different cultures learn different ways of behaving when they are talking with another individual. For example, they learn what topics of conversation are appropriate in different situations, how long to talk at each turn, whether and where to touch a conversation partner, how much silence is acceptable, and many other subtle but very important points. Differences in communicative style often give rise to misunderstanding and disharmony in interactions between foreign students and institutional faculty and staff. Having the knowledge and ability to explain these differences helps FSA's to serve effectively as intermediaries and thus to increase their influence.

Appendix J, taken from the University of Iowa's *Handbook for Foreign Students and Professionals,* discusses "The Communicative Style of Americans" in a way that is intended to be helpful to foreign students.

Describing reactions to the encounter with new cultures

Some scholars have sought to describe, or at least find patterns in, what happens to people psychologically when they enter a new culture. (Examples are the works of Foust and others, Brislin, and Church, all cited in the reference list.) Since foreign students are always in the process of adjusting to a new culture, FSA's can get ideas from these writings that are useful in understanding their clients and helping their clients understand themselves.

Prescribing conduct for improved intercultural relations

Implicitly or explicity, nearly all the writings cited in this section offer suggestions or recommendations for people who want to interact harmoniously with people from other cultures. Brislin has suggestions not just for interpersonal interactions, but for administrators of culture-contact programs. FSA's will want to pay close attention to those ideas, to try them out, and, if possible, improve on them.

Recommended basic bibliography

Learning Across Cultures: Intercultural Communication and International Educational Interchange (Althen) brings together a large number of ideas from the intercultural communication field as they apply to foreign student affairs. There are chapters on adjustment, counseling, training, and TEFL; there are some case studies as well. Each chapter has an extensive bibliography.

Hoopes' and Pusch's introductory essay in *Multicultural Education* (Pusch) is an excellent overview of basic ideas in the field of intercultural communication. And Brislin's *Cross-Cultural Encounters* is laden with interesting ideas and useful suggestions.

An Introduction to Intercultural Communication (Condon & Yousef) offers an array of ideas that will be enlightening for anyone who works with foreign students. The chapters on value orientations, language, nonverbal communication, and "Thinking about Thinking" are especially useful.

Finally, Stewart's *American Cultural Patterns: A Cross-Cultural Perspective* helps FSA's see the natives as the foreign students see them. This is nearly always beneficial. Stewart also offers a framework within which to analyze the cultural value dimension of cross-cultual interaction in general.

Perspective

Whether or not they make an explicit study of intercultural communication and consciously apply their learnings to their work with foreign students, most FSA's operate on the faith that their work will result in improved relationships among representatives of diverse cultures. Those improved relationships are expected to lead in some way to a better world.

The work of University of Chicago geographer Marvin Mikefell raises questions about the validity of this faith. Mikefell wonders whether a propensity toward "culture conflict" is an inherent part of human nature. He defines a culture as a group sharing a language or a religion. He points out that there are almost no single-culture countries in the world. Except for Iceland and two or three other small countries, all other countries contain more than one cultural group. And in all cases there are unsettled relationships between or among them. The degree of disharmony varies in its strength, but, no matter what governments have done to try to include or exclude various groups, disharmony has persisted and violent conflict has not been rare. Is such disharmony and violence inevitable? If it is not, or if its level can be reduced, cultural intermediaries such as foreign student advisers indeed have an important role in the contemporary world. Few people have the opportunities that FSA's enjoy to help people from various cultures learn to understand and respect each other despite their differences.

IMMIGRATION REGULATIONS

Working with immigration forms is usually considered the minimal, essential function of foreign student advising. Virtually all FSA's carry their institution's responsibility for signing immigration forms. Some FSA's do little else. This section of the *Handbook* does not attempt to provide details about immigration law, regulations, or procedures. Information on those matters is available elsewhere, as we will see. The purpose of this section is to provide general guidelines about the immigration-related work of foreign student advisers. We will consider the difficulties of doing that work, FSA responsibilities concerning immigration, and references.

Difficulties

Several factors make it difficult for FSA's to be competent in the area of immigration advising. First, the immigration law itself is extraordinarily complicated. So is the manner of its implementation, which involves several federal agencies in one way or another. Faced with pages and pages of legal language, many people despair of understanding.

Second, there are frequent changes in the law, the regulations, the interpretation of the regulations, and/or the personnel responsible for implementing the law. Keeping abreast of those changes is not easy.

Third, the immigration law gives considerable discretionary authority to INS officers, even those at a rather low level. This means that the law and regulations are interpreted and applied differently by different people. Thus, what is good immigration advice in one INS jurisdiction may be bad advice in another.

Fourth, it seems easy to get misinformation about immigration matters. Many people believe they understand aspects of immigration procedures that in fact they misunderstand (usually because they have overgeneralized from some personal experience), and their misunderstandings are accepted by others.

Finally, the aura of authority that surrounds immigration-related work seems to evoke in some personalities a tendency to try to dominate or control others. It is not unusual to encounter instances where FSA's have gone beyond their responsibilities under the regulations and made unwarranted demands on students who needed a signature on an immigration form. It is very important for FSA's to have a clear conception of what their immigration-related responsibilities are and are not.

Responsibilities

An FSA's formal responsibilities under the law and regulations are minimal; each institution may add somewhat to those responsibilities. The informal responsibilities, which derive from the formal ones, are much more extensive.

Formal. The immigration regulations specify what is required of the "designated school officials" who sign immigration forms. Those regulations change from time to time, and so are not recounted here. The section on references, below, gives sources of current information about the regulations. In general, the regulations require authorized school officials to follow certain guidelines in issuing immigration forms and to make certain reports to the INS about students whose status *vis-a-vis* the institution has changed.

It is important for FSA's to realize that the INS, not the foreign student adviser or the educational institution, is responsbible for enforcing the immigration law. The NAFSA *Adviser's Manual of Federal Regulations Affecting Foreign Students and Scholars* offers very sensible guidelines concerning the FSA's role with respect to immigration matters.:

> It is very important for the foreign student adviser to define carefully for himself and for the aliens with whom he works the area of his responsibility and authority and to stay within those defined limitations. It is clearly the responsibility of the foreign student adviser to ensure that the aliens with whom he works are fully and properly informed and instructed regarding their privileges and responsibilities and regarding the limitations placed on their activities by U.S. laws and regulations. It is also clearly the responsibility of the foreign student adviser to perform in a thorough and professional manner the specific duties assigned to him by the laws and regulations for the particular classes of aliens for whom he has responsibility.
>
> It is just as clearly *not* the responsibility of the foreign student adviser to *enforce* the laws and regulations or to make reports to government agencies which go beyond the reporting requirements specified for each class of nonimmigrant. To do so would be to exceed his authority and responsibility, confuse the administration of the law, and, most important, destroy his working relationship with the aliens with whom he works, thus making him ineffective in his assigned and proper duties. The foreign student adviser must be thorough and professional in carrying out his responsibilities, but he must confine his activities to the area of his authority and responsibility if he is to serve the best interests of the foreign students and scholars he advises and the effective and efficient administration of the laws.

From the point of view of educational institutions, the FSA is usually assigned responsibility for issuing immigration forms in the institution's name and giving whatever guidance and information students need in order to maintain their immigration status.

Informal. An FSA's informal immigration responsibilities can be summarized in this statement:

DO NOT GIVE INCORRECT IMMIGRATION ADVICE

The possible consequences of giving incorrect immigration advice are so serious for the student that FSA's must be very cautious about the advice they give. FSA's will want to be well aware of the limits on their understanding of immigration law and procedure and to be ready to defer answering questions until a correct answer can be given. Or they may want to refer some questions elsewhere. They also need to assure that staff members in their offices are equally cautious about giving immigration advice.

To do their jobs properly, FSA's need to know the purpose of all immigration forms their clients may have occasion to use. FSA's need to know, in addition, when each form can properly be issued and how it is supposed to be filled out.

Knowing the proper use of forms entails knowing the pertinent aspects of immigration law, regulations, and procedures. The extent of the knowledge an FSA will want on these topics depends on the type of institution involved. An FSA at a smaller institution where only F-1 students enroll will need far less knowledge about immigration regulations than will an FSA at a large institution which has an Exchange-Visitor program (and therefore has students and/or staff in J-1 status), students in assorted nonimmigrant categories, and occasion to hire aliens for staff or faculty positions.

At a minimum, FSA's will want to know about the following immigration-related matters:

1. what the Immigration and Nationality Act (usually referred to simply as "the Act") says about nonimmigrants in general, about F-1 students, and about any other category of nonimmigrants the FSA's institution attracts

2. the roles of the INS and the Department of State in the implementation of the Act

3. the relationship between the Act and the federal regulations

4. the procedure by which regulations are changed

5. procedures for obtaining a student and other relevant types of nonimmigrant visas

6. the regulations concerning F-1 student initial entry, temporary departure, extension of stay, transfer from one institution to another, and employment; the regulations on these same topics for other nonimmigrant categories encountered at the institution

7. the regulations concerning change of nonimmigrant status and reinstatement to student status

8. the general structure of the INS

9. district INS personnel and their responsibilities

10. the law, regulations, forms, and procedures concerning adjustment of status (for FSA's who have a role in hiring foreign faculty and staff)

11. sources of information about immigration matters

plus updates

References

FSA's must have the NAFSA *Adviser's Manual of Federal Regulations Affecting Foreign Students and Scholars,* a readable, well-organized compendium of law, regulations, and procedures. The periodic *NAFSA Newsletter* carries up-dates that can be noted in the *Manual* when changes are made. NAFSA tries, furthermore, to distribute information about immigration-related changes through various networks of its members.

There are limits, however, to NAFSA's ability to give rapid distribution to information about legislative, regulatory, and procedural changes related to immigration. FSA's who have more than a few foreign students at their institutions will therefore want to subscribe to the weekly *Interpreter Releases,* compiled by lawyers who specialize in immigration law. The *IR* subscription rate is rather high and most of the material in each issue has no bearing on foreign students, but it is still worth the price. (For rates, write American Council for Nationalities Service at the address given in Appendix F.)

Also useful is the article "The FSA and the INS"(see Appendix K), which was originally written to be a chapter in the NAFSA *Manual* but not included due to funding problems. "The FSA and the INS" can help FSA's understand the situation of INS employees and in other ways can aid foreign student advisers in establishing and maintaining a reasonable working relationship with district INS offices.

The NAFSA *Manual* has a bibliography with entries that will assist those FSA's who want to learn more about immigration matters.

One might suppose that the INS itself would be the best source of immigration information for FSA's, but that is often not the case. The Service has not given high priority to answering the public's questions. Furthermore, most Service employees, if they do have information that might be helpful in a particular case, are under such heavy pressure from backlogged work that they cannot easily give close attention to inquiries from FSA's or other members of the public. FSA's can often get more thoughtful assistance from other, more experienced, foreign student advisers.

It should be mentioned that the instructions printed on INS forms are generally clear and comprehensive. They deserve close attention.

Students and others often inquire about the idea of retaining an attorney for handling immigration cases. When considering referral of an immigration case to an attorney, it is well remember that immigration law is a special subject that most attorneys, even some who call themselves specialists in immigration law, know little or nothing about. Membership in the American Immigration Lawyers Association has only recently begun to require some demonstration of experience in immigration law. No assurance of competence is required.

Thus, the selection of an immigration attorney is best made with great care. Students are well advised to interview more than one attorney before selecting one. FSA's cannot properly recommend certain attorneys in preference to others.

☞6

Skills

Just as good FSA's need to have knowledge of diverse subject matter areas, so do they need an array of skills. Skills can be learned. Reading, formal instruction, informal instruction, guided practice, and careful observation of others (whether they provide good examples or bad ones) are all means of enhancing one's skills. Generally, putting skills to use and then getting others' evaluations of one's performance is the most effective means of developing skills.

In this chapter we will discuss four general areas in which FSA's had better develop skill. They are communicating, administration, education and training, and counseling. This division into four areas is arbitrary, as is the subdivision of some of those four areas into more specific topics. The purpose of this chapter is to identify skills FSA's can benefit from having and to offer suggestions for developing them. In Chapter Seven, "Practices," we will talk about putting one's knowledge and skills into operation.

COMMUNICATING

"He just can't communicate" is a complaint we have all heard. What people seem to mean when they say someone can't communicate is that the person usually cannot convey his thoughts, ideas, or feelings to others. People who "just can't communicate" probably cannot succeed as foreign student advisers because so much of what FSA's do involves making things clear to others. FSA's need to be able to do that. The challenge is all the greater for FSA's because there are so many things they are called upon to make clear to others and so many different "others" to make them clear to.

The term "communication" can be applied to virtually every-thing people do *vis-a-vis* others. The term will be used in a more restrictive way here, referring to interpersonal communication, writing, and public speaking. In any of these applications, as I see it, making things clear to others requires first having them clear in one's own mind. Unless one begins with a clear notion of the thoughts, ideas, or feelings one wants to convey to others, the complaint that "he (or she) just can't communicate" may be appropriate.

Another key component of successful communicating, whether in interpersonal or other situations, is attention to one's audience. Since FSA's are called upon to communicate with such a wide variety of people they need to make special efforts to find ways of sending clear messages.

These and other aspects of human communication are discussed in a helpful and lucid way in David Berlo's *The Process of Communication*, a book any FSA could benefit from reading.

Interpersonal communication

Much of an FSA's work is done in face-to-face interactions with other people. Those people have widely varying backgrounds, varying proficiency in English, and differing communicative styles. In these circumstances, making oneself understood and understanding others require constant effort and attention. FSA's will want to develop skills in:

1. finding out whether others have understood what they intended to say

2. making clear what they have understood others to say (usually by paraphrasing or summarizing)

3. being more or less continuously aware of what is taking place in the conversation (called "the process" in social science jargon)

4. adjusting their manner of presentation (relative to level of English used, the use of written as well as oral messages, choice of examples, extent of self-revelation, etc.) to suit the particular audience

Some of these communication skills have been mentioned already in the section in Chapter Two on self-awareness. It was suggested there that people who want to become more effective in interpersonal communication will need to take a course or participate in an organized program intended to help people improve their communication skills. Reading alone is rarely sufficient, because other people's reactions to one's behavior are needed.

Writing

As administrators, FSA's are called upon to write. At a minimum they have to answer their mail. They normally prepare written information on assorted topics, such as pre-arrival information for newly-admitted foreign applicants, instructions for routine immigration procedures, and newsletters or other messages to students. They also have the usual interoffice memos, and they commonly write reports or proposals for their superiors. Some FSA's, in addition, decide to or are called upon to write articles for publication.

FSA's can be more efficient and effective in their jobs and can be more influential among institutional and professional colleagues if they can write clearly—and, preferably, fairly quickly. The administrator who writes the minutes of the meeting, the report on the study, the position paper on the proposed new policy, or the proposal for the project is often the one best situated to influence the outcome. Skill in writing pays many dividends.

William Zinsser's *On Writing Well* is a good general overview of the craft of writing. Jefferson Bates' *Writing with Precision* gives practical advice to people who want to learn to write better. In *Revising Prose*, Richard Lanham describes procedures for improving something one has already written. Courses in expository writing can help; so can a colleague who writes well, pays conscious attention to the skill, and is willing to act as an editorial mentor.

Many of the deficiencies in the type of writing FSA's do can be avoided by following these few guidelines:

1. Before starting to write, organize the ideas that are to be conveyed. Clear writing is based on clear thinking. In a piece of any length, it is helpful to explain the pattern of organization to the reader. "The purpose of this letter is to. . ." "The first topic is. . ., which leads into a consideration of. . ." "In conclusion,. . ." Etc.

2. Avoid jargon, slang, and fad words. The field of education is notorious for its jargon and use of "new" terms. Recent examples

are "interface" and "pro-active." Make it a rule never to use such words.

3. Avoid the use of the passive voice (for example, saying "It was suggested by Professor Wilson that..." instead of the more lively and direct "Professor Wilson suggested..."). Use of the passive voice is one way in which some people manifest what appears to be a need to make their writing seem formal or official. The actual result of this approach is more often stiff and unnatural wording.

4. Make sure that indefinite pronouns (this, these, those) have clear antecedents, so there can be no doubt in the reader's mind what they refer to.

5. Use no extra words. Make every word contribute to the message that is being conveyed.

6. Reread a completed piece of writing from the viewpoint of a new foreign student who has an intermediate command of English. Would such a student understand what the piece is about and what it says about its subject? If not, modify it until there is every reason to suppose that the new student would be able to understand it. Then other types of readers are likely to be able to understand it also.

Public speaking

FSA's can avoid public speaking, but if they do so they forsake opportunities to develop influence among students, institutional and professional colleagues, and members of the community. Of course, they fail to capitalize on these opportunities if they agree to give presentations and then perform poorly.

Most people are not skilled at public speaking. They seem to start without a clear idea of what they want to convey, or fail to organize their material in a way the audience can readily follow, or neglect to make their presentations interesting. Many people convince themselves that they "can't" speak in public, as though the ability to do so were genetically based. It is not, of course. People can improve their skill in public speaking, and FSA's are encouraged to do so.

Moving Mountains (Boettinger) is among the many books that can be instructive for people who want to develop public speaking skill. Books are not enough, though; as is the case with developing skill in interpersonal communication, there is need for other people's comments on one's performance. Classes in public speaking are relatively easy to find. Toastmaster clubs offer an excellent way to improve one's speaking skill.

Once they have a clear idea of what they want to convey, would-be public speakers need to pay particular attention to the audience they will be addressing. How much does the audience know about the topic to be discussed? How can ideas best be conveyed to them—through speaking alone or with visual aids as well? Is a theoretical approach better, or a practical one? What sort of illustrations are likely to hold interest? Will they consider humor appropriate? Self-revelation?

After they have prepared a presentation, would-be public speakers ought to ask themselves if they would like to be in the audience for their own presentation. Would it hold their attention? Would they learn something from it or be entertained? If not, more work is needed. Simple courtesy requires that a speaker not bore an audience by failing to prepare an interesting presentation.

ADMINISTRATION

FSA's are rarely high-level administrators who are expected to be concerned with long-range planning, formulating large budgets, the development of significant new undertakings, or coordinating large-scale operations. Nevertheless, FSA's can benefit from developing skills in the traditional administrative areas of planning, evaluating, and coordinating. Managing time well and making productive use of committees and of meetings are other administrative skills FSA's will want to foster. Before turning to these topics, however, let us consider a less precise but at least equally important subject—working within a bureaucracy.

Working within a bureaucracy

Whether they work in smaller or larger institutions, FSA's are in hierarchical structures with certain reporting channels, job descriptions, and routine procedures for getting things done. The advantages and disadvantages of the bureaucratic form of organization have long been discussed and debated and no doubt will continue to be. Whatever one's views on this topic, the fact is that FSA's can be more successful if they learn how to work within the confines of the bureaucracy, changing (or at least trying to change) the way the bureaucracy works when it seems necessary to do so.

It is difficult to offer specific guidelines or instructions for working within a bureaucracy. Institutions and situations differ so much from each other that it is hard to generalize. *The Peter Principle* (Peter & Hull)—a witty and insightful book—and *Up the Organization* (Townsend) offer some useful ideas, as do some of the time management books mentioned later in this chapter. Some other ideas are presented here.

Attitude.   People who are oblivious to matters of bureaucracy and people who feel constrained and resentful when they must act within the confines of a particular niche in a hierarchy are generally handicapped in administrative positions. There may be one exception to this. That is the case of a person who has been hired to "shake things up," to reorganize, redirect, or build a significant new program. Such a person may need to defy the norms of bureaucratic behavior.

FSA's are not usually supposed to be what some call "movers and shakers." They are much more often expected to operate according to normal organizational procedures. Given that expectation, they are probably best equipped to function effectively if they adopt the attitude that the bureaucracy is a reasonable form of organization, one in which beneficial ends can be accomplished by people who are patient, persistent, and skillful at working within its confines.

People who work in bureaucracies had better fully accept and act upon the idea that it is their supervisor's job to answer their questions and respond to their requests. I have encountered many FSA's who express reluctance to "bother" their superiors with requests they know will be unwelcome. I think that view leads to inaction, ineffectiveness, and festering discontent. A more appropriate view is, "I know that my boss won't want to hear about this, but it's my job to bring it to her attention, and her job to do something about it. I wouldn't be doing my job if I didn't raise the issue, and she would not be doing hers if she didn't do something about it. If she doesn't like to hear about things like this, that's her problem, not mine." (Cf. the discussion about problem ownership in Chapter Four.)

This is not to say that matters of timing and approach should be disregarded. They need attention. Issues can be raised at better and worse times and in better and worse ways. An effective administrator will raise them, though, rather than try to ignore them.

Knowledge.   To reiterate: FSA's, and anyone else who wants to work effectively in a bureaucracy, must know the institutional structure. They must know or be able to find out the locus of authority for decision-making on any matter that may arise. FSA's, for example, need to know who makes decisions on such matters as registration procedures, how the institutional seal can be used, and what variations in student billing or fee payment procedures can be allowed. Without this knowledge, FSA's cannot put their bureaucratic skills into practice.

Skills. The skills required for working in a bureaucracy are far easier to list than to elaborate upon, because the manner of their implementation varies so much from institution to institution and from situation to situation. Most of these skills, it will be clear, require making judgments that take many factors into account.

1. Acting within the scope of one's authority, not exceeding it (by making promises one is not empowered to keep, for example, or approving things one is not empowered to approve), *or* failing to act within one's authority to its fullest extent (by referring clients elsewhere for matters that one is expected to take care of oneself). To help in making judgments as to whether or not a particular matter is within the scope of one's authority, one can ask, "Am I the proper person to make the decision that is needed here?"

2. Including superiors in questions that involve policy or ethics (as opposed to the implementation of settled procedures). Ask, "Do we have a routine way of dealing with this or does it raise issues that need the attention of people with more authority than I have?"

3. Consulting others whose approval or participation would be needed for the implementation of a given decision. For example, consulting with the housing officer before telling a sponsoring agency that your institution could accommodate 20 new students next term. Ask, "Can I implement this decision myself or would I need someone else's agreement or participation to do so?"

4. Going through channels—that is, referring to the appropriate person, via the proper organizational route, those matters of which one cannot dispose independently. Ask yourself, "From whom does the person whose action is needed on this receive requests (or orders) to take action?" Remember that the organizational route to a person who is above oneself in the hierarchy, or who is in a different chain of command, is normally through one's own superior.

5. Keeping others informed about what you are doing or have done, and about evolving matters of interest to them. Ask, "Who would want or need to know about this? Would it be to my

advantage (as the FSA) if someone knew about this?" Memos, carbon copies of correspondence, meetings, and reports are the conventional ways of keeping people informed within a bureaucracy. FSA's usually find it to their advantage to have people above them in the hierarchy (all the way to the top, if possible) informed at least in general terms of what they do and what issues they face.

6. Writing down important things—as an aid to memory, a record of decisions made or advice offered, and a basis for the handling of subsequent, similar cases. Ask, "Is it absolutely clear that it would be a waste of effort to have notes or a record about this?" Unless the answer is positive, then write something down. I have been amazed at the number of instances when I have been inconvenienced, hampered, or perceived as inept for failure to have kept notes about some interaction that seemed trivial at the time it took place.

7. Being persistent and patient. Worthy things can be accomplished in a bureaucracy. Perhaps not today or this week, but eventually. Persistence and patience—combined with influence—can make things happen.

Planning

FSA's commonly lament that "All I do is put out fires. I never have time to do anything creative or even to think about what I am doing." It is indeed often the case that foreign student offices are understaffed and overworked. The development of certain administrative skills can help FSA's avoid being full-time firefighters or to escape that condition if they want to. Planning is one of those skills.

How planning helps.   Having a plan gives an FSA something to work toward, some basis for the establishment of priorities. The activity of planning forces one to think about the future and anticipate changes it might bring. FSA's, however busy they may be, do have spare moments at the office, and in the shower, when they could be thinking about or working toward some longer term objective. Without such an objective in mind, however, those spare moments are likely to be spent thinking about that day's fires.

How to plan.   One need not do an elaborate needs assessment survey to find out what improvements institutional colleagues and foreign students would like to see made. Ask a few of them for their opinions and recommendations. What problems recur? Improved instructions or information might reduce the incidence of routine problems. What procedures take too long and are boring to carry out? Maybe they could be streamlined. What situations represent potential for learning but are not being exploited? A new program might be designed. What would you like to experiment with and spend more time doing? Think about ways to do it. What external conditions (e.g., an increase in the enrollment of students from Country X or a budget cutback) will require changes in the way things are now being done? Devise ways of making those changes.

After accumulating a number of ideas for projects to be carried out over the next year (the usual time frame for planning in U.S. organizations), rank them. There is nothing scientific about that process. Consider such factors as urgency, the importance of pleasing the people who suggested the various ideas, practical matters such as the availability of time and space, and personal preferences. What emerges is a set of objectives for the year, in order of priority.

Following through on the plan.   List the steps needed to accomplish the top two or three objectives. Schedule time each week (or some other relatively brief period) to take those steps. Schedule time each month to review the progress made on the realization of the plan. Fifteen minutes per month to review progress is often enough for the review.

It helps to inform one's superior of the plan and of progress toward its implementation. That adds incentive to work on it. (In some cases, of course, the superior mandates that planning be done.)

At least once yearly, schedule time (there are some remarks later about time management) to evaluate what has been done.

Evaluating

Evaluation can be more or less elaborate. George Renwick, in his *Evaluation Handbook*, offers many ideas about the systematic evaluation of cross-cultural projects, and those ideas are often generalizable to other kinds of undertakings. Sometimes a few informal questions addressed to students or institutional colleagues (for example, "Does this problem come up as often as it used to?") will provide all the evaluation that is needed to decide whether a particular problem or subject matter area needs additional attention. Sometimes mere reflection is all that is needed to get an evaluation. The point is that evaluating what one is doing is an inseparable part of doing a good job, but does not have to be arduous.

In some institutions, periodic evaluations are a part of normal administrative procedures. FSA's might be given guidelines for evaluations of their own offices or be subject to reviews conducted by others within their institutions.

Coordinating

In the literature about management and administration, the term "coordination" usually refers to the activity of assuring that the various people or organizational units under one's supervision are working harmoniously together toward common aims. Some FSA's are in a position to be concerned with coordination of this type, but most are not (except, perhaps, insofar as they themselves are the subjects of someone else's coordinating). Most FSA's are concerned with coordination of another and probably far more difficult type. They need to try to assure that all the people and offices in their institution are working harmoniously together toward having a sound foreign student program. This is difficult because, among other factors, FSA's have no power over many (or even any) of the people whose work they are trying to coordinate.

How can FSA's proceed when they are faced with the task of coordinating the work of people who are not responsible to them? That is what this *Handbook* is about. FSA's need to develop influence on their campuses by bringing to bear the characteristics, ideas, knowledge, and skills being discussed in these pages. First, though, they need to accept two important assumptions:

1. FSA's cannot hope to develop high quality foreign student programs at their institutions on their own. There is too much to do, and too many other people have roles in what needs to be done. The FSA, again, is an intermediary and an informal leader.

2. Coordinating takes time, patience, and attention to detail. The temptation to do things oneself because it is simpler must be resisted.

Operating on the basis of these assumptions and employing the suggesions offered throughout this book, FSA's can set out to coordinate their own efforts with those of their colleagues.

Time management

Busy administrators who do not want to spend all their time fighting fires have to learn to manage their time well. There are a number of useful books on this topic, so we will not go into the subject in detail here. Some books I have found useful are *How to Get Control of Your Time and Your Life* (Lakein), *The Time Trap* (Mackenzie), *How to Put More Time in Your Life* (Scott), *Getting Things Done* (Bliss), and *Get It All Done and Still Be Human* (Fanning & Fanning). I recommend buying at least three of these relatively inexpensive paperback books, reading one each nine months or so, and then reviewing them periodically after that. This approach helps in developing and maintaining good time use habits. The maintenance part is important, because people tend to regress into sloppy practices.

Most people find a number of reasons (excuses) for not committing themselves to improving their time management habits. The principle explanation FSA's offer for not modifying their time use habits is that they cannot adopt any practice that would limit their availability to foreign students. They know that time management authorities all recommend scheduling times that are kept free from interruptions. "I can't do that," many FSA's say. "A student may need to see me."

FSA's who cannot overcome the assumption that they must be accessible to students at virtually any time will always be firefighters. Reading, writing, planning, evaluating, and coordinating are all activities that require some concerted attention, free from interruptions. It took me about two years as an FSA to realize that. Then I began scheduling one day each week when I had no appointments, took no telephone calls, and locked my office door. No disaster ensued. As I now explain to people (foreign students and others) who express dismay at having to wait a day (or maybe longer) in order to see me: "No foreign student ever died or got deported because he couldn't see Gary Althen on any given day."

Making productive use of committees

Committees, like bureaucracies, have advantages and disadvantages. Wise FSA's will recognize the advantages of committees, seek their establishment when appropriate, get themselves placed on pertinent committees (at least in an *ex officio* capacity), and develop the skills needed to profit from committee work.

Committees, especially ones mainly concerned with foreign students, can perform several functions that are valuable for foreign student advisers. The functions include:

1. providing a forum for disseminating information about specific foreign student-related issues or problems or about the institution's foreign student program

2. providing a source of ideas, reactions, and suggestions from disinterested colleagues

3. lending legitimacy to acts that might otherwise be attributed to the FSA personally (such as decisions about financial aid or admission)

4. adding weight to proposals or recommendations that might otherwise come from the FSA alone

5. involving in the foreign student program institutional colleagues who might otherwise have no occasion to develop an interest in or informed opinions about students from other countries

6. providing a basis for the formation of constructive informal relationships with institutional colleagues

To realize these benefits, most FSA's will favor the existence of a faculty-staff (and student, if that is in the institution's tradition) committee to serve in an advisory capacity to the foreign student office or as a forum for discussing foreign student matters. These committees seem to work best when their membership includes representatives of the various offices that work regularly with foreign students and some additional, disinterested staff or faculty members. An individual's membership on these committees is best limited to some fixed term. Otherwise there is the risk of stagnation or the development of unhealthy vested interests.

Once such a committee exists, FSA's will want to develop skill in assuring that it functions well. This skill has the following components:

1. providing members with the background information needed to understand the committee's role and any issues the committee confronts

2. working informally with the committee's chairman to assure that each meeting is well planned and that the chairman has the information and sense of direction needed to conduct a good meeting

3. working informally with any committee members who appear to need additional information in order to understand some issue the committee is treating or some encouragement to take a more constructive role in the committee's work

A final point about these committees needs to be made clear: The FSA cannot usually guarantee that advisory committees will work well or accomplish their intended objectives. It happens that certain mixes of people do not work. There can be clashes of personality, viewpoint, or style that disrupt a committee's operation. Members cannot be compelled to be interested in the committee's work, so some may remain silent or may not attend meetings. Or the chairman, even though an admirable and very capable person otherwise, may not be skillful at conducting meetings. That skill is our next topic, and the final one of this section on administration.

Making productive use of meetings

As administrators, FSA's spend considerable time in meetings. That can be dreary in the extreme, because most people are not skilled in leading meetings in a way that makes them interesting, productive, and enjoyable. Nor are most people skilled in being constructive participants in meetings other people lead.

Conducting meetings takes skill, and so does participating in them in a constructive way. FSA's can make their own lives more interesting and at the same time increase their influence if they are able to run meetings well and to help other people's meetings be efficient and fruitful.

Learning to make productive use of meetings can begin with reading, but, like the development of other skills, requires actual practice followed by evaluation from other people who see the performance. Some institutions offer meeting leadership workshops or short courses. In the absence of such formal opportunities for developing the skill, an interested group can put together its own short course, using readings and films about conducting meetings (consult a film catalogue), and scheduling practice meetings in which the participants give constructive critiques of each other's performances.

In *Leader Effectiveness Training,* a book I think any FSA could benefit from reading, Thomas Gordon offers (on pages 127-135) a number of useful suggestions for people who are responsible for conducting meetings. Another widely used book about conducting meetings is *Taking Your Meetings Out of the Doldrums* (Schindler-Rainman & Lippitt).

Common flaws in the conduct of meetings include the failure to have in mind or make clear to the group what the meeting's purpose is; the absence of priorities among the various items before the group; bringing up (or allowing to be brought up) matters that are not appropriate for the particular group; failure to keep discussion relevant to the topic under consideration; and failure to make a clear decision about each item that is considered. People who conduct meetings are well-advised to see it as their responsibility to make their meetings as interesting and fruitful as possible. That is not always easy, because some topics are boring to nearly everyone and some meeting participants staunchly engage in counterproductive behavior. Meeting leaders can at least partially compensate for these difficulties by exhibiting enthusiasm and a sense of purpose concerning their meetings. In addition, they can try to follow these guidelines:

1. Accept the responsibility for leading. Do not let a fear of seeming authoritarian or undemocratic interfere with fulfilling the group's need for leadership.

2. Make sure the topics to be discussed are appropriate for the particular group attending the meeting. The topics should be relevant to the interests of all or nearly all group members and within their area of competence and authority.

3. Know just what is to be accomplished at the meeting. Cut off any discussion that detracts from accomplishing that aim.

4. Have an agenda, one that is either prepared in advance or developed at the outset of the meeting. (Members are best given an opportunity to modify an agenda that was prepared in advance so that the agenda is not seen as one imposed by the leader.) Follow the agenda. Cut off any discussion not aimed at treating the item under consideration.

5. Reach a clear decision on each agenda item. This may mean that a particular person is assigned to carry out a particular task by a certain date. Or it may mean that the item is referred elsewhere, dropped from further consideration, or placed on the agenda for a subsequent meeting. (To conclude consideration of an item by saying, "Well, let's all think about this and we'll discuss it later" is not likely to produce a positive result or a favorable reaction to the leader.)

Most meetings have only one leader (at least formally), but many others in attendance. Gordon (pp. 136-138) lists these responsibilities for people who are attending meetings lead by others:

Before the meeting, (1) reread the minutes of the previous meeting, (2) arrange to avoid being called out of the meeting, (3) plan to get to the meeting on time, (4) have your agenda items in mind, (5) have background information for your agenda items ready, (6) study the agenda if it is available in advance, and (7) inform and prepare your alternate if you cannot attend.

During the meeting, (1) submit your agenda items, clearly and without elaboration, (2) state opinions and feelings honestly and clearly, (3) stay on the agenda item under consideration, and help others to do likewise, (4) ask for clarification when you need it, (5) participate actively, (6) make contributions that will help the meeting move along, such as asking questions, summarizing, and clarifying others' statements, (7) encourage silent members to participate, (8) listen to others, (9) think creatively about solutions, (10) avoid disruptive communications such as sarcasm . . ., and asides, (11) keep notes on what you agree to do after the meeting, and (12) keep saying to yourself, "What, right now, would help this group move ahead. . .? How can I help. . .?"

These suggestions about leading and participating in meetings are much more effectively put to use by people who have some of the characteristics and skills discussed in this *Handbook*, particularly self-awareness and the ability to communicate well in interpersonal situations. It also helps meeting leaders and participants to have some sense of the manner in which groups typically operate (called "group process" in the jargon of social psychology). Various schema for observing and analyzing group process are available (see, for example, those by John Jones and Philip Hanson). These schema draw attention to such matters as competition for leadership, the various ways leaders and members can contribute to a group's functioning (by summarizing, for example, or clarifying a point), and various ways in which leaders and members can interfere with a group's work (for example, by digressing, not paying attention, or making personal attacks on other members). People who are aware of these and other aspects of group process can almost always exert a beneficial influence on meetings because they can see the problems in the process and take steps to allay them.

EDUCATION AND TRAINING

Facing mounds of paperwork and a string of student clients, FSA's sometimes have to stop and think to realize that they are not—or need not be—just firefighters and paper-pushers. They have an educating and training role. They acquire knowledge and skills in the intercultural relations area that are unusual, important, and potentially helpful not just to foreign students, but also to American students, institutional personnel, and people in the community.

FSA's function as educators and trainers in many of the things they do involving foreign students, including orientation programs, workshops on intercultural relations, pre-departure workshops, counseling (the subject of our next section), and the daily interactions where they are trying to help students manage their affairs in a more constructive way.

FSA's might also organize and conduct orientation or other programs for community volunteers and for institutional staff who work with foreign students. Most FSA's also have occasion to train personnel in their own offices.

To do this education and training well, FSA's need to develop a number of skills, some of which have aready been discussed in other contexts:

1. *Clarifying objectives.* Education and training programs, if they are well conceived, begin with a clear notion of what it is that is to be conveyed.

2. *Selecting and combining appropriate approaches.* There is a long list of methods for use in education and training program on intercultural relations. Lectures, films, exercises of many sorts, written information, role plays, case studies, and critical incidents are among them. It requires skill to select methods that are appropriate for a particular purpose and a particular audience and then

combine them in a sequence that has some logic and that holds participants' interest.

3. *Conducting training exercises.* In many of the programs they conduct, FSA's provide guided practice for the participants. To do that they need skill in conducting training exercises and discussions. This entails knowing the purpose of the activity, giving clear instructions, answering questions clearly, encouraging reticent participants, drawing pertinent points from any discussion, and curtailing digressions.

4. *Public speaking.*

5. *Writing.* Written materials are more effective, of course, if they are well organized and clearly written.

6. *Evaluating.* People who organize educational and training activities usually want to have an idea how well they have done and how they might do better next time. Those ideas come in part from evaluations of the programs they conduct.

Once again we will offer here the names of some useful publications, but not before reemphasizing the point that skill development requires practice. FSA's who want to build skills in education and training can sometimes find appropriate programs at their own or nearby institutions. They can pay close attention to the design and conduct of programs in which they themselves are participants. And they can often arrange to work as an assistant to a more experienced program director.

"Cross-Cultural Training" (Pusch and others) presents a clear introductory discussion of the formats in which FSA's may find themselves working as trainers. It offers a step-by-step guide to designing a program, discusses various training methods, and gives suggestions for evaluation. It concludes with an extensive bibliography.

Multi-Cultural Education: A Cross-Cultural Training Approach (Pusch) provides very clear instructions for the use of many exercises that experience has shown to be effective in training programs.

Robert Kohls' *Developing Intercultural Awareness* offers a well-designed, 13-module program for Americans wishing to learn something about intercultural relations.

I believe that FSA's who want to conduct effective education and training programs in cross-cultural relations also need to verse themselves in the readings cited in Chapter Three on the subject of intercultural communication.

It is not just in formal programs or sessions that FSA's serve as educators and trainers. They also do so in their work as counselors.

COUNSELING

Counseling seems to be a particularly troublesome area for many people who work with foreign students. FSA's are not usually trained counselors and many of them work at institutions where there are no trained counselors on the staff. Those FSA's who do have institutional colleagues certified to do counseling are sometimes reluctant to refer foreign students to them because FSA's have come to suspect that U.S counselor training usually does not prepare people to counsel clients with foreign cultural backgrounds.

An interest in "cross-cultural counseling" is beginning to grow but has yet to produce much that is especially practical. *Counseling Across Cultures* (Pedersen and others) is a recent compendium of articles on the subject. A relatively brief and provocative overview is in the Horner & Vandersluis chapter on "Cross-Cultural Counseling."

None of what appears in this discussion of counseling is intended to suggest that foreign students frequently and freely approach FSA's to ask for counseling. They rarely do. They usually take problems elsewhere, if they do not simply try to cope with them on their own. FSA's are more likely to become involved in counseling by chance in their routine dealings with students or when students with problems are referred to them by colleagues or other students. Troubled students sometimes visit the FSA to ask routine questions, seemingly hoping their troubled condition will be noticed and then discussed. FSA's and their clerical staffs ought to watch for students whose attitude or demeanor bespeaks a problem more serious than the one being voiced.

It seems to me that there are a number of misconceptions that commonly cloud people's reactions to the notion of trying to help people, especially foreign students, who are perceived to "need counseling." People are likely to be considered in need of counseling when they are behaving inappropriately or are experiencing prolonged unhappiness and/or some other negative feelings.

Misconceptions

One misconception, it seems to me, is that counseling is a mysterious process, particularly if the person being helped is culturally different. I would certainly not say that human beings are simple creatures whose emotional disorders are readily understandable and easy to repair. But there is a mystique surrounding "counseling" that tends to make the activity seem to be reserved for those with special training. Some training might help some people become more effective as counselors, but it does not always do so. And many untrained people are very effective at helping others with their personal problems. Stephen Rhinesmith, writing for host families of foreign students, put it well:

> The chief thing to remember is that the best way to approach a counseling session is to feel natural and relaxed. Counseling should be something you enjoy and take up easily. You should do it because you have a real concern about people and you care about them in a way that enables you to empathize with them.

A second misconception, fostered by the manner in which counselor training is carried out at many U.S. institutions, is that effective counseling is essentially a matter of always saying the right thing at the right time. Over and over again, students of counseling are presented with situations or partial scripts of counseling sessions and then asked, "What would you say next?" This approach, it seems to me, leads to an overemphasis, at least among newly-trained counselors, on particular statements and particular questions. It draws attention away from the overall atmosphere surrounding the counseling session and the general relationship between the counselor and the client. (And it overlooks the possibility that the client might prefer not to have the counselor say anything, but rather to wait silently for the client to continue speaking.)

A third misconception follows from the second. It is that dire consequences will follow from one bad response. "But what if I say the wrong thing?" the would-be counselor asks, trembling slightly.

I would not argue that what a counselor says is unimportant. I would say that there are other and more important aspects of the counselor-client relationship, especially the establishment of mutual respect (not necessarily liking) between the two. If a client believes a counselor is respectful and earnestly trying to help, the counselor can say some "wrong" things and nothing horrible will happen.

A final misconception has to do with foreign students in particular. There is a widespread assumption, it seems to me, that foreign students are psychologically fragile and that their cultural backgrounds are somehow sacred. These assumptions together lead to a coddling of foreign students, an unwillingness to confront them when their own attitudes and behavior are causing them problems. I have seen too many foreign students persevere through too much difficulty for me to be able to see them as unusually delicate and vulnerable.

Further, it is clear that some culturally-based behaviors do not transplant to another environment and need to be changed if the client is to be able to realize valued objectives such as the completion of a course of studies or the establishment of satisfying social relationships.

Skills

The skills needed for counseling foreign students are not, in my view, different from those needed for counseling native students. What is different is the need for *awareness* of the effect of cultural differences on the entire enterprise. We will look at the topic of awareness in a moment; first we will look at two counseling skills, *listening* and *giving helpful reactions*.

Listening. I have been struck again and again by the number of times foreign students have sat in my office and told me at length about a serious problem or set of problems they were experiencing. Then, before I had even begun to decide what I might say in response, they have smiled, said "Thank you very much for listening to all this," and left. All they wanted was to be listened to.

Of course, many students want or could benefit from more than being listened to. But good counseling starts with good listening. "Good listening" is perhaps too simple a term, suggesting as it does the mere absence of impediments to hearing what another person says. Good listening entails much more than that. It entails letting the other person know (or feel) you are accepting and respectful, that you are interested, and that you understand or are trying to understand what is being said to you.

Good listeners, then, have the characteristics of patience, respect for others, and nonjudgmentalness that were discussed in Chapter Three, and the interpersonal skills discussed earlier in the present chapter.

Gordon uses the term "active listening" to label the activity we are discussing here. His description and guidelines, in his book *Leader Effectiveness Training*, are well worth reading.

Giving helpful reactions. The unfortunately vague term "giving helpful reactions" is used here to encompass the wide variety of responses a counselor might offer a client once the client has made the problem clear. Reactions might include any or several of the following (which appear in no particular order of importance or appropriateness):

1. questioning to get a more comprehensive understanding of the client's problem, situation, past history, behavior, opinions, feelings, or tentative solutions

2. offering support and understanding

3. providing information the client seems to need

4. challenging the client's assumptions, information, or analysis of the situation

5. telling something relevant about one's own experience or viewpoint (called "self-revelation" or "self-disclosure" in counselor parlance, and often less benefical with foreign clients than with domestic ones)

6. suggesting a course of action or alternative courses of action

7. helping the client to devise a set of possible courses of action and to choose from among them

8. suggesting or teaching an alternative way of viewing the situation

9. commenting on the apparent reasonableness of the client's behavior or feelings

10. formulating a "contract" in which the client agrees to undertake some modification of behavior

11. remaining silent or otherwise encouraging the client to continue talking

12. referring the client to another person or agency presumably better qualified to help

What makes counseling an art rather than a science is the fact that no formulas can be offered for choosing from among these various responses (let alone saying just how to word each one). A would-be counselor must hope to develop a sense for what is—or seems to have the best chance of being—helpful to the particular client at the particular time. At the very least, the counselor needs to be able to judge when a response has not been helpful and to have something else to offer.

It is worth emphasizing that the twelve types of response listed above are those familiar to Western counselors and therapists. Other approaches can be found elsewhere. The Naikan method and Morita therapy, for example, are used in Japan. Under the Naikan method, a client spends several days or even a week or more in complete isolation from other people or stimuli. The object is intense and prolonged introspection. Morita therapy begins with a period of absolute bed rest, again in isolation from outside stimuli. Then comes a period of physical work (Lebra).

Both the Naikan and Morita approaches have as their object reinforcing the client's sense of interdependence with and obligation to other people. Western approaches rarely have that goal.

Awareness

Counselors who help people who are culturally different need to be aware of the effect of cultural background on the counselor-client interaction. We have already (in Chapter Three) suggested three aspects of human behavior that are affected by cultural background: assumptions and values, communicative style, and patterns of thought. Cultural differences in each of these areas have some bearing on a counselor-client interaction. Here are a few of the matters about which the counselor and the client may differ:

1. ideas about the sources or origins of emotional disturbance
2. ideas about the manner in which emotional disturbance is best treated (if indeed it is to be treated at all, rather than merely accepted)
3. ideas about the individual's role in creating and solving personal problems
4. ideas about the likelihood of getting useful help with personal problems from a stranger

5. the amount of self-disclosure considered appropriate between strangers with certain status differences
6. nonverbal communication habits
7. turn-taking in conversations
8. forms of reasoning that are convincing

The best an FSA can do, it seems to me, is to be aware of these and other dimensions along which culture causes people to be different from each other. FSA's cannot hope to know the assumptions and values, the communicative styles, and the patterns of thought that predominate in all the cultures their clients represent. (They may, in the course of a longer term counseling relationship with a particular client, learn a good deal about that particular client's cultural background.)

In "Counseling Students with Unrealistic Academic Objectives," my colleague Fran Stott and I discuss some culturally-influenced factors that counselors will want to hold in awareness when counseling foreign students whose academic aspirations seem unattainable. The factors relate to the genesis of the problem, forces that cause it to persist, and means of approaching it in a counseling relationship.

In addition to having the skills and awareness discussed here, it seems to me that it is helpful for counselors to adopt some conceptual framework for analyzing a client's problem and deciding how to proceed with the counseling. Students of counseling are exposed to an array of schools of thought about counseling. Psychoanalysis, reality therapy, transactional analysis, gestalt therapy, non-directive or client-centered therapy, and Adlerian psychology are examples. (In *Current Psychotherapies*, Corsini collects readings concerning twelve different approaches to the treatment of emotional disturbance.) In some programs students of counseling are urged to adopt one or another of these approaches as their own; in others they are encouraged to develop their own "eclectic" approach.

My approach

Handbook readers who are familiar with the various contemporary American approaches to counseling will have recognized the influence of Albert Ellis on these pages. Ellis is a psychologist who labels himself the father of what he calls Rational Emotive Therapy, or RET. Ellis's ideas stem from the Greek philosopher Epictetus, who Ellis frequently quotes as having said, "Men are disturbed not by things but by the views which they take of them." The essential notion is that people's feelings stem not so much from what happens to them as from the ideas they have about what happens to them. Ellis argues that most people have many "irrational" ideas which, when applied to what happens to them, cause them to upset themselves. To get rid of the upset, one attempts to get rid of the irrational ideas. Ideas, after all, can be changed.

Ellis claims great efficiency for RET. My own experience using RET with students, colleagues, and myself bears out his claim. With RET, one quickly gets at the client's irrational ideas, shows how those ideas are really the problem, and helps the client learn to "dispute" them and replace them with rational ideas. In the process, the client usually learns the RET approach well enough to be able to apply it without the aid of a counselor.

RET commends itself to use with foreign students on at least three grounds. First, it is highly directive. In general, foreign students seem less responsive to the non-directive methods many American counselors prefer; they want teaching and direction. RET offers it.

Second, RET seems to be less based on the individual-as-the-center-of-the-universe assumption that characterizes most U.S. approaches to counseling. While it rests on the way a particular individual thinks about things, it recognizes consideration of others as a legitimate criterion in decision-making.

And third, RET is particularly effective with verbally-oriented people. College and university students, at least foreign ones in the United States, are usually such people.

I would not want to suggest that all FSA's adopt the RET approach. It would not suit all their personalities. But I would urge them to investigate it and give it their consideration. *The New Guide to Rational Living* (Ellis & Harper) is the most widely read explication of RET. I think *Humanistic Psychotherapy* (Ellis) is more helpful to people who would use RET in counseling. *Growth through Reason* (Ellis) contains transcripts of RET counseling sessions. *Reason and Emotion in Psychotherapy* (Ellis) is the most thorough discussion of the theoretical basis of RET. The last chapter, which offers a large number of reasons why Ellis believes human beings are predisposed to emotional disturbance, is particularly interesting.

Most of Ellis's own writing is addressed to a lay audience. Three of his associates—Susan Whalen, Raymond DiGiuseppi, and Richard Wessler, have written *A Practitioner's Guide to Rational Emotive Therapy*, an almost jargon-free book that would help anyone employ RET.

Learning counseling skills

For FSA's who can begin to learn skills from reading books, I strongly recommend the following:

Parent Effectiveness Training and/or *Leadership Effectiveness Training* (both by Gordon)

Humanistic Psychotherapy and *Growth Through Reason* (both by Ellis)

A Practitioner's Guide to Rational Emotive Therapy (Whalen, DiGiuseppi & Wessler)

Microcounseling (Ivey & Authrer)

Ivey's main concern is what he calls "microcounseling," the development of listening skills (he calls them "attending skills") and the ability (it must be said) to appear interested in and respectful of other people.

Ivey markets videotapes that are intended to help people develop attending skills and also "influencing skills," which are ways of offering the helpful reactions discussed earlier in this section. For information about Ivey's tapes, write Microtraining Associates, Inc., Box 641, North Amherst, Massachusetts 01059.

Ellis also markets tapes and films. For a catalogue, write the Institute for Rational Living, 45 East 65th Street, New York, N.Y. 10021.

Other tapes and films for counselor training are listed in film catalogues.

Courses and training institutes in counseling are often available through universities and elsewhere. Information can be obtained from the counseling department (or whatever it is called) at any major university.

☞7

Practices

THIS CHAPTER SEEKS to provide detailed suggestions for dealing with several aspects of an FSA's work: aiding foreign students, promoting culture learning, administering an office, and pursuing professional development.

AIDING FOREIGN STUDENTS

At a minimum, FSA's are expected to assist foreign students in overcoming obstacles that may hinder them in the pursuit of their academic objectives. Typical FSA activities are discussed here under the headings of admissions, orientation, housing, financial matters, health insurance, advising and counseling, handling emergencies, immigration advising, general problem-solving, liaison activities, working with student organizations, community relationships, programming, and relations with foreign alumni. In all of these areas it is important to remember that people from different backgrounds are likely to have different notions of what constitutes "help." A foreign student seeking an FSA's help may expect the FSA to provide information, list alternatives, recommend a certain course of action, offer emotional support, personally carry out some task on the student's behalf, and/or intercede for the student with some other individual. Sometimes FSA's need to ask a student, "What is it that you would like me to do in this case?" The FSA may or may not be able to accede to the student's wish, but at least both will have a clear understanding of each other's expectations and limitations.

Admissions

FSA's have a keen interest in foreign admissions, because (1) the institutions' policies on foreign admissions do much to shape the

96

overall foreign student program, (2) the applicants who are admitted become the FSA's charges, and (3) many matters that come to the FSA are, at least in part, admissions matters. FSA's and foreign admissions officers have common interests in institutional policy regarding foreign students, administrative arrangements for dealing with foreign students, evaluation of academic credentials, transfer of academic credit, financial eligibility of applicants, assessment of English proficiency, orientation of new students, academic advising, foreign students' success, relationships with other institutional offices and personnel who deal with foreign students (e.g., the registrar's office and the business office), data collection, relations with academic departments and faculty, relations with sponsoring agencies, relations with foreign alumni, and staff training and development.

FSA's had better be intimately familiar with the admissions procedures of their own institutions, whether or not they have direct responsibility for this function. Furthermore, they will want to know something about the fundamental aspects of foreign admissions in general. This includes credentials evaluation, TOEFL scores, and documentation of financial resources. NAFSA's *Selection and Admission of Foreign Students* provides a good overview of a foreign admissions officer's concerns. And, of course, FSA's can learn about foreign admissions through conversations with people who do that work.

It is prudent to have a mechanism whereby the FSA, if not responsible for admissions decisions, is routinely notified of the admission of any foreign applicant. The FSA can routinely receive a copy of the Certificate of Eligibility, and preferably of the letter of admission as well. It is good for the FSA, for counseling purposes, to have a copy of each student's application form and, particularly, documentation of financial support. As discussed in NAFSA's *Orientation of Foreign Students*, newly-admitted foreign applicants should be sent pre-arrival information covering a number of topics, such as transportation to the campus, housing, and costs. Whether this information is mailed by the admissions officer or the FSA, the FSA will normally have much to say about its contents because it is the FSA who deals with new students and is therefore in the best position to judge what pre-arrival information might be useful.

FSA's will want some way, formal or informal, of letting admissions officers know how those foreign applicants who do arrive are faring. Is this group doing exceptionally well? Or poorly? Are individuals in certain circumstances consistently having academic or financial problems? Admissions officers need information of this type in order to make adjustments in their requirements or procedures.

Clearly, then, FSA's and admissions officers need to work closely together if both are to do their own jobs and serve their institutions well. There is often a formal arrangement, such as membership on a foreign student committee or regularly scheduled meetings, to assure that FSA's and foreign admissions officers have an adequate forum for sharing information and ideas. Sometimes informal relationships suffice.

A harmonious relationship between the FSA and the foreign admissions officer (if they are different people) can do much to enhance an institution's foreign student program and at the same time make the professional lives of the two individuals less stressful. It seems to be the case, though, that FSA's and foreign admissions personnel at given institutions often see things differently, have significantly different values, and do not get along well. It is desirable for both to try to understand each other's viewpoint and to develop a relationship based on mutual respect. In cases where the FSA-foreign admissions relationship lacks harmony, it may be worth calling on the services of a third party to serve as a consultant or mediator in helping establish a more constructive relationship.[1]

Orientation

NAFSA's *Orientation of Foreign Students* coupled with the chapters on adjustment and training in my *Learning Across Cultures* provide a substantial base of ideas and information for FSA's who are designing or conducting orientation programs. Both publications discuss what to include in an orientation program, and how to present it.

Orientation is usually considered a basic function of FSA's, to the point that others often hold unrealistic expectations of it. Some people seem to believe that if everything that "should" be covered in an orientation program is in fact included, then there will be no

[1]In *Managing with People,* Jack Fordyce and Raymond Weil provide some specific guidelines for meetings designed to improve the working relationship between two people. In my experience these methods work.

problems with foreign students. It is not like that at all, of course. FSA's need to devote significant energy to orientation, be ready to modify their approach if that seems warranted, and then explain from time to time that no orientation program can anticipate and solve all of everyone's problems. Nor can newly-arrived foreign students be expected to comprehend and absorb the enormous quantity of information that orientation programs typically provide.

Housing

Having a suitable place to live is a major concern of foreign students. They usually expect FSA's to render as much help as possible—or more help than is possible—in that area. Of course, FSA's will want to offer as much aid as they can. This entails (1) providing comprehensive information about the kinds of housing available, the difficulties in finding housing, and the costs; (2) providing information upon the students' arrival about means of finding housing, contracts and leases, and the advantages and disadvantages of the different kinds of housing available (if indeed there is more than one); and (3) actual help in locating housing, whether offered personally, through the institution's housing office, or by volunteers.

For many students, having a foreign roommate proves to be a memorable educational experience. FSA's who want to promote culture learning encourage foreign-American roommate arrangements, whether in residence hall rooms, in international wings or houses, or in off-campus lodging. Beyond that, they will want to encourage the development of reasonably open relationships between U.S. and foreign roommates. Providing copies of my *Learning with Your Foreign Roommate* is one way to do that. Holding workshops or at least culture learning sessions with roommate pairs (or trios, as the case may be) is another way. Additional ideas about culture learning are discussed later in this chapter.

Financial matters

Unless an institution enrolls only very wealthy students from countries that remain free of major disruptions, some of its foreign students are likely to encounter financial difficulty. So, unless an institution has an unlimited supply of financial aid, the FSA is going to have to deal with foreign students' financial problems. Following the guidelines given here can reduce the incidence and severity of these problems:

1. In all information sent to foreign applicants about the institution, provide complete estimates of the cost of attending. Specify items and the cost of each: tuition, housing, vacation housing, food, books, insurance (about which more is said below), transportation, incidental expenses, and any other items that can reasonably be anticipated. Allow for inflation, and state that costs can increase.

2. Require documentation from applicants showing the availability of adequate financial support. Include a statement, to be signed by the applicant, affirming that funds in the designated amount are or will be available.

3. When newly-arrived or recently-arrived students say they do not have enough money, tell them the institution cannot help. Point to the information the institution supplied about costs and to the student's own signature on the financial verification form. Explain that the institution made every effort to inform the student of the costs of attending and to assure that the student had enough money, and it simply cannot accept responsibility for students who do not heed the information.

4. Have an emergency loan fund, with formal, written procedures governing its use. No matter what precautions are taken, situations beyond students' control will arise and they will run short of money. It is the consensus of those in the field of international interchange that institutions admitting foreign students have an obligation to assist in cases of genuine, short-term financial emergencies. The written information about the loan fund should cover eligibility, application procedures, and terms for repayment. The existence of this formal policy helps control abuse and the appearance of favoritism.

5. If it seems necessary, special arrangements might be made for delayed tuition payments, payment of tuition in installments, or other concessions to the restrictions on sending dollars from certain countries. If such arrangements are made, it is prudent, again, to have written policies concerning eligibility and other details.

It is important for FSA's who work with students' financial problems to internalize the idea of problem ownership (see Chapter Four). FSA's simply cannot solve all foreign student financial difficulties, however worthy those students might be. Sometimes worthy foreign students are victims of circumstances that make it necessary for them to interrupt, if not abandon, their academic programs.

Health insurance

One of the most difficult things for foreign students to comprehend is the amazingly high cost of medical care in the United States. Foreign students often fail to understand the importance of getting health insurance.

The NAFSA Board of Directors has recommended that institutions require foreign students to buy health insurance if it is administratively feasible to institute such a requirement. (And if it is deemed legal. Some institutional attorneys have advised that requiring health insurance of a particular group of students would be illegal. Other attorneys have disagreed. At this writing there is no court opinion on the question.)

If health insurance cannot be required, it is sensible to use every imaginable means of encouraging and even cajoling students into buying it, not just for themselves but for their dependents as well. If there is no institution-sponsored insurance policy available, then one or more of the policies designed for participants in international educational interchange programs can be used. (See the advertisements for these policies in any issue of the *NAFSA Newsletter*.)

FSA's are often compelled to learn a bit about comparative medical care delivery systems and about the workings and terminology of the American insurance business in order to answer students' questions on the topic.

Advising and counseling

The initial posture. Many texts and courses in counseling place considerable emphasis on the manner in which the initial contact between the counselor and the client takes place. What is involved is "establishing rapport" with the client. This is described as showing friendliness, a modicum of cheerfulness, and genuine interest in the client. I question this prescription. The genuine interest needs to be there, as has already been said, but I believe that FSA's are best advised to withhold that characteristic American friendliness and cheeriness until they are certain that it suits the client's frame of mind. I believe that an emotionally neutral, businesslike approach to each client is preferable.

I was present once when a graduate assistant working in my office encountered a foreign student who had come in for an appointment. "Hello!" was the graduate assistant's cheerful greeting. "How are you doing? Just fine, I hope."

Had the student not been doing just fine, it would have taken great courage to say so. The cheerful and optimistic greeting would have kept many students from bringing up an unpleasant, unsettling, or embarrassing subject. A death in the family, problems with an adviser or a roommate or a girlfriend, a poor grade on an exam, gnawing questions about whether to return home soon or stay on for another degree—these and many other topics that are on the minds of many foreign students are far less likely to be expressed to an FSA (or even a secretary) who is unremittingly cheerful. A more neutral opening is probably more appropriate and even more respectful.

Giving advice.   An FSA, the title implies, is a person who gives advice. But there are persistent warnings that we all hear as we grow up: "Never give advice." "There's no point in giving other people advice, because they do what they want to anyway." Our experience tends to confirm that giving others advice is futile. Others need to make up their own minds about what they will do, and having advice they do not want to follow can only make the decision more complicated. Following someone's advice and then having the matter turn out unfavorably can damage the relationship between the giver and the receiver of advice.

Much of the "advising" FSA's do is not really advising in the sense of telling others, or at least suggesting to them, what they ought to do. Often FSA's are simply *explaining or interpreting* things to students. What does a particular business office form mean? Why do fellow students seem so reluctant to share their class notes? Explanations and interpretations can be offered without giving advice.

Sometimes FSA's are just *supplying information*, another activity that can be separated from giving advice. "These are the policies on . . . ." "Here is how that procedure works."

FSA's sometimes help students *reflect* on something. Assistance of this sort means just listening, paraphrasing, and helping students make sure they have thought of all the relevant aspects of the issue and have them in some reasonable perspective.

Students sometimes benefit from help in *listing alternative courses of action.* "I'm about to graduate. What should I do?" This activity often entails giving information ("Here is the procedure for applying for practical training permission."), explaining, and helping students reflect. It might also entail something else FSA's often do, and that is *estimating the likely outcomes* of various possible courses of action. Such estimates can be based on the FSA's knowledge and judgment, but need not be in the form of advice. "In my experience, students who do that usually . . . ." "Whether that will work depends on . . . ."

There are few situations in which FSA's actually seem called upon to give advice, in the sense of saying something like, "Here's what you should do: . . ." I reserve that phrase for times when it seems very clear to me that there is only one prudent course of action open to the student and failure to follow that course is very likely to have negative consequences. "You should buy health insurance." "You should send that application form now if you want a response by the end of the term." "You should go to the dinner and get there on time, if you accepted the invitation." And so on.

When students press me for advice about what to do in a particular set of circumstances, I will usually not be any more directive than to say, "If I were in that situation, I think I would . . .," and then explain why I would do it. I try to convey to students the notion that *they must decide,* that the decision is not mine. I furthermore try to convey the sense that *it does not matter to me what decision they make.* This, it seems to me, is the natural—and constructive— outcome of having a clear notion of problem ownership and of being respectful and nonjudgmental toward students. "Giving advice" is best restricted, in my view, to situations where the FSA clearly knows more than the student, is in a better position than the student to make the judgment, and the student clearly wants and is open to following the advice.

Passing the buck. FSA's are frequently presented with problems or questions that must be referred elsewhere. The registrar has to decide, or the business manager, or the instructor in the course. When a student's problem or question needs to be referred elsewhere, the FSA can do a variety of things. The choice among them depends on several factors, including at least these:

1. the student's English proficiency
2. the student's apparent psychological readiness to deal with someone other than the presumably sympathetic and patient FSA
3. the estimated likelihood that the person who must actually deal with the issue will understand it adequately if the student conveys it (Does the student understand it in the first place?)
4. the other person's receptivity to foreign students (Is she kind and reasonable? Is she a bigot?)

Taking all these factors into account, FSA's can do anything from telling the student, "Don't worry, I'll take care of the whole thing," to saying, "Go see the registrar." My own inclination is to encourage students to do as much as they possibly can for themselves. When referring students elsewhere, I find it helpful to give them a piece of paper on which I have written the name and office address of the person to be seen. If the question to be asked seems complicated, it is helpful to write down suggested wording. If it is likely that the person who makes the decision will need background information the student cannot supply as readily as the FSA can (for example, about the general problems of getting dollars from Country X), the FSA might call the other person to explain the background or give the student a note to take along.

Following through. Their "advising" often leaves FSA's with follow-up work to do: write a letter to the embassy; call the business office; get information about that procedure; etc. FSA's gain influence if they follow through on such commitments promptly and capably.

Saying "no". Desirous though they may be of helping foreign students in every possible way, FSA's will encounter instances in which it is necessary to decline a student's request. Some FSA's find it difficult to say "no" to a student. This may be attributable to the FSA's strong desire to be a "nice person," truly dedicated to helping students from abroad. The difficulty in saying no may also stem from a desire not to be the one who bears the bad news, implements the harsh policy, takes the hard line, or brings the dream to an end.

Some student requests, though, would require actions or decisions that are impractical, illegal, against the institutions' policies or rules, or against good practice. The wise FSA will firmly deny these requests.

One common example of a request that should be denied is for a letter affirming something that is not true. The student may "absolutely need" a letter saying that he is enrolled full time when he is not or that he is studying engineering when he is not or that he is getting better grades than the record shows. The student may need such a letter "just this once." It is wrong, unprofessional, and often illegal to attest to untrue statements. Disastrous personal and professional consequences can result from knowingly making false statements.

Another fairly common request that should always be denied is for a signature on a blank form. The potential for abuse is simply too great to make the risk worthwhile. Requests for personal loans, or for co-signing for loans, are also best denied in all cases.

A less specifiable sort of request that also ought to be declined is one that may aid the student in the short run but will, in the longer run, produce even greater difficulty. Approving short-term loans to a student already hopelessly in debt is one example. Helping an academically inept student change majors is another. When it becomes clear that a student is on a course that will end unhappily, it is better to help the student face up to the difficulty than to prolong it by granting a request that will simply delay the day of reckoning.

Saying "no" often requires saying the word "no" itself, sometimes repeatedly and even loudly. When we say no to fellow Americans, we often do so in rather indirect ways. We say such things as, "I really don't think that could be done in a case like this." Or, "That's not what our policy says." Americans may recognize these gentle ways of saying no. Non-Americans may not; indeed, they may interpret them as invitations to negotiate. Many foreign students are more practiced negotiators than Americans are, so when negotiation starts the foreign students often win. Negotiating is much less likely to occur in the first place if the student's request has been answered with a clear, unequivocal "no."

Say no with authority. A denial or negative response coming from a person who appears unsure or tentative is much more likely to be challenged, especially if the request is for something the student perceives as important. Sometimes it is possible to *anticipate* the need to say no and to say it before the question is actually asked. "Since you are registered for only eight credit hours, we can't give you a letter saying you are a full-time student." Sometimes it is helpful to move quickly to a discussion of what *can* be done: "But we can give you a letter saying simply that you are a student here."

It is usually appropriate and helpful to explain in full why a negative response is being given. This may entail an explanation of the institution's policy on a given point, or of the political factors involved in a decision (for example, why a public institution cannot devote millions of dollars to financial aid for students from other countries). If a rational explanation for the no is not offered, or if the FSA saying no does not appear to be acting in a rational way, the student may suppose the FSA is being arbitrary or unfair. The student is then likely to take the question to another person who is perceived to be more fair or more "interested in students." Students deserve a simple, rational explanation for denials of their requests.

Another way to account for a "no" is to refer to the FSA's *role* in the situation: "I do not have the authority to issue the kind of statement you want."

If there is an avenue for appealing the FSA's negative decision, the student should be told about it in full. The student should be told who can hear the appeal, in what form (oral or written) the appeal can be made, and what criteria will be applied in consideration of the appeal.

It may be more difficult for female than for male FSA's to say no convincingly, since many students come from places where females are not in a position to deny important requests. Female FSA's can confront this openly: "You may not think someone who is a woman can make a decision on a matter like this. But I can. It is the foreign student adviser's job to make decisions about requests like yours, and I am the foreign student adviser here."

In making their requests for actions the FSA deems unwarranted or improper, students will frequently try to get the FSA to feel responsible for solving the problem—to "own" it, in other words. As has already been said (in Chapter Four), FSA's will want to avoid accepting ownership of students' problems. If the student has a financial problem, for instance, it is best kept clear that the student has the problem, not the FSA. The FSA will want to help and will do so if possible. It may not be possible to offer anything other than sympathy, though, and the student may be left with a problem. That happens. The FSA might discuss ways of confronting the problem—transferring to a less expensive school, borrowing money from a distant relative, or even leaving school.

Many students have the idea, probably based on considerable experience, that they can get what they want from an institutional official by mere persistence—asking and asking until the official gives in. If indeed the answer to a student's request ought to be no, then the FSA ought not to say yes just to avoid seeing the same student yet again about the same request. The FSA might say such things as these: "We have already discussed this. Unless you have some new information for me, there is no point in discussing it again." "If you keep coming back to see me about this same thing, the secretary and I are likely to get angry. It probably won't help you if the secretary and I get angry." "I will not want to discuss this anymore unless you have some new information about the situation."

None of this is to say that an FSA cannot be sympathetic to students with problems. On the contrary. But FSA's cannot accede to just any request from just anyone without destroying their own influence and ability to be effective. They need to be more concerned about their general standing within the institution than about the feelings of an individual student.

Handling serious counseling cases. FSA's, however well prepared they may be as counselors, will not be able to treat all cases of emotional disturbance that might arise among their clients. Suicidal or manic behavior and persistent paranoia are examples of problems most FSA's cannot handle. They are faced with the need to get help from a "mental health professional." Unfortunately, such help often seems unavailable. Either there are no certified counselors or psychiatrists in the vicinity, or those who are present cannot be assumed to have the awareness needed to work constructively with students from other countries. Financial problems often further complicate these situations.

When these cases arise, FSA's, in my opinion, have two principal responsibilities. The first is to do everything possible to try to keep the students from hurting themselves or others. This is likely to entail referring the student (and maybe taking the student personally) to whatever professional help is available, even if it means traveling some distance and even if the desired awareness of cultural factors seems absent. FSA's themselves sometimes have to sign papers to commit students to mental institutions. In these cases, FSA's probably have to take the view that the students may or may not be helped by the professionals, but they are more likely to be helped by them than by an FSA or someone else without appropriate training. And at least they will be prevented from hurting themselves or others.

The second thing FSA's usually want to accomplish in these serious cases is to get the student home, because long-term treatment of emotional disturbances is expensive in the United States and usually less effective than it could be at home. Getting the student home is likely to involve contacts with the student's family and, perhaps, with the appropriate embassy or consulate. In these instances—and sometimes in less serious counseling cases as well—FSA's may want to call on the student's friends or compatriots for help of kinds that would not be needed with native students. FSA's and counselors or psychiatrists might need the help of a student's fellow nationals for understanding the student's problem from the perspective of the student's culture; for ideas about the way the case might be handled at home; for communicating with the student in a language the student knows better than English; and/or for communicating with the student's family. If the student has no known friends among fellow nationals, then FSA's can work with nationality group leaders to get the necessary help.

In my experience with cases of serious psychological problems among foreign students, the expense issue ultimately becomes irrelevant. If the case is serious enough, the student will get some care even if there is no insurance or other provision for payment. Care will be offered before a mentally disturbed person will be left free to do bodily harm.

Handling emergencies

FSA's are normally expected to assume an active role in emergency situations that involve foreign students. These may be deaths, serious illnesses or injuries, or arrests. It is not always clear what FSA's ought to do in these cases, and, again, different audiences may have different expectations about that. In general, it is reasonable for the FSA to do what the afflicted student's family would presumably do or to see that some other responsible person does them.

In the case of a death, the next of kin and also the student's embassy should be notified. The FSA may be the one who arranges a funeral or the transportation of remains to another country. The FSA may be the one to send a student's belongings home and take care of the affairs of an estate.

In the case of injury, illness, or arrest, it may be prudent to delay or forego notifying the family, depending on the student's wishes and the prospects for the family's taking some constructive action in the situation.

When students are arrested, it is important to assure that they have qualified legal assistance.

FSA's can usually get help in dealing with emergencies that involve foreign students. The student's friends and fellow nationals may be eager to assist. Fellow nationals from a nearby city might become involved if there are none closer by. Student service organizations, insurance agents, hospital personnel, community service organizations, legal aid societies, churches, the Red Cross, and embassy or consular officials might also be asked to assist.

FSA's ought to have in each student's file a form on which the student has given the name, address, and telephone number of the next-of-kin and, when possible, of a relative or acquaintance who is in the United States. When handling an emergency, it is wise to keep a log of all activities, including dates, people talked to (and their telephone numbers), information conveyed, and decisions reached.

Immigration advising

Advising on matters involving the Immigration and Naturalization Service deserves special attention because of its importance in the FSA workload and its special significance to students. The main point about immigration advising has already been made and is repeated here:

DO NOT GIVE INCORRECT IMMIGRATION ADVICE

We have already (in Chapter Five) discussed what FSA's will want to know about immigration law and procedures. In this section are a few practical suggestions about dealing with students on immigration matters.

It is helpful to have written handouts on routine immigration procedures such as re-entering the United States after a temporary absence, applying for practical training permission, and applying for permission to work off-campus. Having these handouts saves staff time and serves students better by providing needed information in a form they can study as often as needed.

Students very often misunderstand their own immigration status. Before answering students' immigration questions, FSA's will want to make certain that the students' situations are clearly and mutually understood. Then they can begin to consider procedures that might be appropriate.

It is prudent to take notes on immigration advising sessions, recording in the student's file the topic(s) of discussion, the alternatives considered, and the conclusions reached. These notes often prove handy in later sessions with the student.

FSA's had better use care in the issuance of any immigration form. This entails making sure that the appropriate form is being used, that the student is eligible to receive or use it, that it has been filled out completely and correctly, and that it is being sent to the correct place. Retaining photocopies of completed forms in the student's file can help answer questions or resolve problems that may arise later, as can maintaining a log of all forms sent to the INS.

As mentioned earlier, developing as constructive a relationship as possible with district INS personnel is crucial to success in immigration-related work (see also Appendix K). It often helps if FSA's approach their dealings with the INS as they approach any other cross-cultural experience. Patience, open-mindedness, the constant effort to see things as the other person does—these are helpful ingredients in dealing with the INS. This topic is pursued later in this section under the heading of "liaison."

Frustration with the INS sometimes leads to the temptation to try to pull strings, usually by requesting help from the local member of Congress. Some congressmen (their local staffs, actually) are more effective than others in getting information or action from the INS. INS personnel rarely appreciate congressmen's involvement in a case, because it can disrupt the normal order of things and it requires extra time and effort. In the interest of developing a long-term, constructive relationship with the district INS office, FSA's will want to be quite circumspect about seeking a congressman's involvement in a case or encouraging others to call the congressman's office.

General problem-solving

Many times each week students bring their FSA's assorted problems for which they want a solution. The variety of these problems is enormous. There are complaints about neighbors, allegations of racial discrimination, incorrect bills, overdue bills, misunderstandings with landlords, disagreements with teachers or roommates, and on and on. Sometimes it is the other party to the problem, not the foreign student, who brings the situation to the FSA's attention.

Whenever these problems involve more than one person, the first thing to do after getting a clear understanding of the complainant's viewpoint is to find out how the other person sees it. That person's view is almost always different from the complainant's, sometimes so different that the two people seem to be talking about different situations altogether. (Frequently FSA's can locate no "truth" between or among divergent perceptions of a problem. If they cannot tolerate that ambiguity, they are likely to add to the problem rather than help resolve it.)

After hearing from both (or all, if there are more than two) parties, FSA's can decide whether to assume a mediator role or an advocacy role. As mediators, FSA's place themselves between the parties to the situation and try to help them find an agreement or a resolution. FSA's work as mediators when they judge that neither side represents the side of goodness, and both have some legitimate or at least understandable demands, wishes, or feelings. Roger Fisher and William Ury's brief *Getting to Yes* offers extraordinarily useful suggestions for negotiating differences. The authors point out the deficiencies of the usual "positional bargaining" approach, in which one party makes an offer and the other accepts, rejects, or makes a counter-offer. In its place they propose "principled negotiation," which sets the two parties side-by-side in a joint effort to solve a mutual problem. FSA's can use the approach described in *Getting to Yes* not just in helping clients negotiate differences with others, but in many other aspects of their work.

When they judge that one side clearly represents the side of right, FSA's can serve as advocates for that side, trying to persuade the other side to go along.

In my experience, mediating is the role most commonly assumed.

Fairly often it turns out that there is no problem. There has been some misunderstanding which has lead to the impression that a problem exists, but once the misunderstanding is cleared up the apparent problem has vanished.

If there is a problem, FSA's will want to make clear to students what authority they have and do not have (usually they have none) in the matter and what they propose to do about it. Following through on what they say they will do contributes to the development of influence.

Liaison activities

Liaison activities represent an important part of an FSA's work. Some of this work is done within the institution and some with external organizations. Those two categories will be discussed separately here, but they have much in common. Both call on the same characteristics, knowledge, and skills described earlier. Both are best done with conscious attention to the other person's viewpoint and situation. In both cases, it is well to try to establish good working relationships *before* some problem or issue arises.

Two of the objectives of liaison work are essentially the same with respect to liaison within the institution and liaison with external agencies. Those objectives are making things easier for foreign students and making things easier for FSA's. Liaison work within the institution has the additional objective of helping institutional colleagues gain the knowledge and develop the skills needed for them to work constructively with students from other countries.

Liaison within the institution. In the previous chapter we discussed committees as one means of maintaining communication among people in the institution who work with foreign students. Other means include periodic informal meetings in each other's offices; lunch meetings; periodic meetings with each other's office staffs; joint attendance at social functions; sharing printed information; and formal sessions designed to convey information about students from particular countries (cf. Appendix I) or about some particular aspect of foreign student affairs (e.g., English proficiency testing or intercultural communication).

Sending formal thank-you letters to helpful colleagues, along with carbons to their supervisors, is nearly always a good idea.

It is beneficial not just for FSA's but also for their staff members to be acquainted with their counterparts in other offices. FSA's can arrange for their assistants, secretaries, and/or student employees to meet with their counterparts in those offices with which they interact and share information about the respective offices' structures and operations. Meetings such as these can produce constructive personal relationships *and* mutual understanding of viewpoints.

When an institution has other offices with an international focus, such as an international programs office that works with faculty, the FSA will want to maintain liaison with personnel there. While the work of the two offices may not overlap, there will be a common interest in the development of institutional and community support for international activities. Cooperative efforts in that area are easier to arrange if a cordial relationship between the offices already exists.

Liaison with external agencies. FSA's work with an array of external agencies, including the INS, other U.S. governmental agencies, foreign governments, and non-governmental sponsoring agencies.

1. *Liaison with the INS.* Appendix K says much on this important topic. Maintaining a constructive perspective on working with "the Service," as INS personnel often refer to it, is one of the biggest challenges foreign student advisers face. Some FSA's routinely phone the INS with their questions, believe what they are told (if they can get through when they call), and assume a pseudo-law enforcement agent posture *vis-a-vis* their students. FSA's who take this stance probably minimize the amount of stress they feel in their relations with the INS. They also minimize the amount of influence they have with foreign students at their institutions.

Probably more numerous are those FSA's whose feelings toward the INS are not positive. They have trouble getting through to the Service, either by phone or in the mail; they are unable to get clear answers to their questions; they get incorrect answers and guidance; procedures take too long; papers get lost; and/or INS employees may be less patient than the FSA would like. Sometimes it seems that an aspect of immigration law or procedure is blocking a seemingly worthy student from realizing a seemingly worthwhile objective. FSA's confront all of these problems.

As the concluding lines of "INS and the FSA" (Appendix K) suggest, much of what FSA's can do to manage their relationships with the INS is to adjust their own attitudes. After all, the INS is a law enforcement agency whose employees can—and do—behave according to their own perceptions of the proper way to carry out their responsibilities. FSA's need to learn as much as possible about immigration law and procedure so they can advise students well, ask intelligent questions of the Service, and understand the answers. After that, FSA's need to work very hard at understanding the situation INS employees face, including the complex nature of the law they are trying to enforce, the remarkable demands on their time, their limited opportunities to get training, their archaic record-keeping systems, and the number of lies they have all been told by aliens and their native supporters anxious to get some immigration benefit. People who work in that kind of situation deserve all the patience and understanding FSA's can muster.

When Service employees do perform in a way FSA's can appreciate, written messages of gratitude, with a carbon copy to the District Director, are a good idea.

2. *Liaison with other U.S. government agencies.*   The biggest problem FSA's face in relating to such agencies as the Visa Office (Department of State), the United States Information Agency, The Department of Labor, the Internal Revenue Service, and the Social Security Administration is knowing where to direct their questions. Most of these agencies are large, and their personnel and telephone numbers change frequently. FSA's at smaller institutions can often turn to their colleagues at larger universities for help in finding out where to direct particular questions. The local offices of members of Congress are another source of help in getting answers from Washington agencies. Some of these agencies have representatives at NAFSA conferences, where FSA's can meet them, record their names and numbers, and get information about where to direct questions.

The Federal Bureau of Investigation and the Central Intelligence Agency sometimes ask FSA's for information about particular foreign students or scholars. Most institutions have written policies restricting the dissemination of information about students, whether to law enforcement agencies or other parties. FSA's should confer with their institution's attorneys before responding to FBI and CIA requests.

3. *Liaison with other governments.* As is the case in dealing with large U.S. government agencies, the major problem in working with other governments' embassies and consulates is usually knowing who to ask for particular information.

FSA's usually need to rely on the telephone in their dealings with embassies and consulates, because letters often evoke tardy replies or none at all. A clerical person at an embassy or consulate will usually know where a particular question should be addressed. Telephoning person-to-person is often the best way to get through if the embassy or consulate is one where staff members are sometimes away from their desks. It is a very good idea to make notes on these telephone conversations, recording the name of the person spoken to, the date, and any agreements that are reached. A follow-up letter confirming the details of the conversation is usually a good way of giving the exchange an appropriate degree of formality and helping assure that it is remembered at the other end.

4. *Liaison with non-governmental sponsoring agencies.* In this context, non-governmental agencies are those which sponsor foreign students in the United States—IIE (Institute of International Education), AAI (African-American Institute), and so on. In dealing with them, the FSA is often an intermediary between an agency staff member and the agency's students at the FSA's institution.

From the viewpoint of the sponsoring agencies, FSA's are the people on the scene, the ones on whom the agencies must rely for complete, up-to-date information on the students' situations.

Agency personnel appreciate FSA's who (a) take the time to become familiar with their students, (b) evidence respect for the students, (c) notify the agency if any special problem develops with a sponsored student, (d) recognize the agency's right to information about students it supports, (e) have good rapport with the faculty, (f) refer students' questions about the agency's procedures to the agency if there is doubt about the correct answer, and (g) refrain from criticizing the agency in a student's presence.

When sponsored students get into a difference of opinion with their agencies, FSA's will usually want to stand aside and let the students and the agencies interact directly with each other. Being in the middle as a channel for messages is rarely efficient or helpful.

FSA's have many occasions on which to explain a sponsoring agency's role and operations to students, since students often misunderstand what the agencies do. In particular, students often suppose that decisions about such important matters as extensions of programs or changes in field of study are made by the agencies, when in fact they are made by the home country organizations on whose behalf the agencies are working.

FSA's will want to remember that personnel turnover at the lower levels of some sponsoring agencies (the title is usually "program officer") is relatively high. And program officers often have large caseloads and limited experience working directly with students on a specific campus. Keeping these factors in mind can help FSA's appreciate program officers' situations, and explain these situations to students.

Working with student organizations

Working with foreign student organizations is a continuing source of frustration for many FSA's. Whether the organizations are based on nationality (e.g., Indian Student Club), regional origin (European Student Union) or a cosmopolitan idea (an international student club), FSA's are unlikely to obtain benefits equal to the efforts they expend. It is important to understand the reasons for this. The most important, from what I have seen in visiting various campuses, is that foreign student advisers' expectations of these groups tend to be unrealistically high. FSA's often begin with ill-founded assumptions about the ease with which these organizations can be formed, then add unrealistic ideas about what the groups can accomplish, and end with an overestimation of their ability to influence them. Let us look at each of these points.

FSA's seem inclined to make one or more of the following questionable assumptions when they are thinking that there *should* be effective foreign student organizations on their campuses:

1. That the foreign students see themselves as an identity group, with enough common characteristics and interests to make it reasonable to form an organization.

The category "foreign students" is usually much more salient in the minds of the Americans than in those of the foreign students themselves. To the latter, differences in language, politics, religion, and even age and field of study are likely to be quite important and to serve as barriers to the development of organizations.

2. That those students who agree an organization is a good idea agree, further, as to what the organization's goals should be (agree, that is, on the degree to which the organization should seek educational, political, and/or social objectives).

In fact, any group of foreign students is likely to include people with quite diverse ideas about what the goals of any foreign student organization ought to be. Bitter disputes over these differences are not rare.

3. That a group of students can readily reach agreement on such matters as purposes, forms of organization, leadership selection, decision-making procedures, and divisions of labor. The article in Appendix D analyzes many of the problems that arise in these areas. The problems stem from culturally-based differences in such matters as communicative style, ways of thinking about problems, and the treatment of differences in social status.

These common FSA assumptions, in sum, appear to be very questionable at best and are often clearly without foundation.

What can foreign student groups accomplish if they are formed? Many FSA's have these ideas: They should (1) develop smoothly running organizations, with easy transitions from one year to the next; (2) provide for many of the social needs of their members; (3) help newly-arriving foreign students get situated and oriented; (4) be able to integrate with American students in the organization for mutual "enrichment"; (5) organize "cultural programs" from which Americans will learn something about the countries the students represent; (6) represent the foreign students, or segments of them, to the institution's administration; and (7) either avoid political activities altogether or at least restrict them to unobtrusive expressions of opinions the local people can be expected to consider reasonable.

Some of these objectives are incompatible with others. For example, activities that would meet foreign students' social needs are likely to be incompatible with activities that would integrate American and foreign students. Some objectives, particularly those involving extensive cultural programs, fairs, performances, and the like, simply expect too much from a group of people whose main purpose in being at school is usually academic success. Some objectives overlook the generic problems of student organizations, especially the lack of consistency in leadership and uneven motivation to participate.

FSA's also frequently suppose they will have more influence on foreign student groups than they are in fact able to exercise. When foreign students do form vital organizations, it usually means, almost by definition, that the members have a purpose or small set of purposes on which they agree. Often that purpose is the propagation of a particular political viewpoint; many times it is to provide relaxed social occasions for a particular language group. Additional or alternative purposes promoted by the FSA are not easily accepted.

In working with student organizations, then, FSA's first ought to examine their assumptions and probably lower their expectations. Taking a longer view they can, with patience and perseverence, seek ways in which they can help foreign students—and maybe some domestic ones too—learn useful lessons from forming (or at least trying to form) organizations of their own.

Here are some things FSA's can do to support foreign student organizations:

1. provide information about the institution's regulations and procedures for forming "official" student organizations and aid the students in complying with those procedures

2. identify prospective student leaders and meet with them to give encouragement and offer support

3. provide information about means by which a nationality group or international club can identify prospective members, raise funds, communicate with members, publicize activities, and better achieve its own goals

4. make clear what assistance the FSA or others in the institution can provide, in the form of money, administrative support, meeting space, audio-visual or other equipment, publicity, leadership training, and so on

5. help students see the lessons that arise from their organizational experiences, even if those experiences do not always have the outcomes the students themselves or the FSA would like

There are important lessons to be learned from efforts to get groups of people to work together cooperatively toward common ends. The efficiency and productivity many foreign students admire in the United States are products of a fairly widespread ability to cooperate in the framework of various sorts of organizations. Experiences with student organizations can induce students to examine their own and their compatriots' ideas and feelings about joint efforts with others.

Programming

FSA's are usually considered responsible for mounting assorted programs that involve foreign students in some way. International fairs and festivals, nationality nights, meals from different countries, tours, and assorted social activities are common examples. Programs of these kinds are traditional on many campuses and may routinely attract large audiences or numbers of participants.

For guidance on the logistical aspects of program planning, FSA's can refer to Barr & Keating's *Establishing Effective Programs* or similar publications. These materials, which are probably available from colleagues in the student activities area, give thorough guidelines on such matters as figuring out the objectives of an event, reserving space for activities, arranging for equipment, getting publicity, holding rehearsals, and so on. A list of "Programming Considerations" appears in Appendix L.

As long as FSA's have the time and ability to do what programming they want, and as long as the programs are more or less "successful," no serious questions about the FSA's programming role are likely to arise. But if the FSA has more and more competing demands and finds it ever more difficult to invest time in programming, or if the programs that are done are not deemed successful, some important questions can come to the fore. Those questions concern the goals of foreign student programming, its audiences, and the FSA's role in the activity.

Goals of programming. While most programs have a combination of goals, one or another goal is likely to be considered paramount. The main goal of a foreign student-related program might be educational or social. The program might be intended to train participants. Or it might be intended to provide beneficial publicity for foreign students, the FSA's office, and/or the institution.

Of course, a program's goal is the first thing to consider in deciding what kind of program to develop. An educational program might include an expert in some discipline or a documentary film. A social program may need music and refreshments. And so on. When planning programs, or assessing past ones, FSA's will want to determine just what they are trying to accomplish.

Audiences for foreign student programs. Programs for foreign students might have one or more of several audiences, including foreign students themselves, American students, faculty and staff at the institution, or the general public. Once again, different sorts of programs are better suited to different audiences. FSA's will want to judge which audiences are most worthy of their limited attention and work on programs aimed at them.

The FSA role in programming. Perhaps the most difficult issue in programming is determining what role the FSA ought to play. At some institutions, FSA's or their staff members assume a very active role. They determine what programs are going to be carried out, reserve the rooms, send the invitations, set up the tables, and so on.

Other FSA's leave these matters entirely to other people, perhaps student groups or perhaps institutional staff members whose main responsibility is student activities. Between these extremes are those foreign student advisers who lend support or advice in some form, or cooperate in assorted ways with other offices, but refrain from direct involvement in programming.

There is obviously no correct answer to the question about the FSA's proper role in programming. In general, it is probably advisable to rely on others as much as possible. It is better to rely on students in order that they might have the experience of planning and implementing an organized activity. It is better to rely on colleagues so they can become increasingly involved with students from other countries. More is to be learned that way, and the FSA's attention can be directed to matters with which other people are less able to help.

Community relationships

FSA's have educational and political reasons for cultivating relationships with members of the community. For educational reasons, FSA's will want to maximize the number of opportunities for constructive interaction between foreign students and people in the community. Host family programs, public schools programs, home visits, and foreign student participation in community service and recreational programs are all means whereby students and community members can learn from each other.

Politically, FSA's have an interest in the development of a constituency knowledgeable about and supportive of international educational activities. Community programs contribute to the development of such a constituency. And community programs can work to combat the development of open anti-foreign sentiments and actions of the kinds that have culminated in violence in some U.S. communities during the past few years.

The development of community programs requires considerable patience and perseverence, because the programs normally depend on the efforts of volunteers. Interested, capable volunteers need to be identified, given gentle direction, and supported in as many ways as possible. Some volunteers have motives FSA's cannot approve, such as religious or political proselytizing or an unhealthy need to compensate for some perceived deficiency in their personal lives. Handling such situations requires considerable attentiveness and tact.

Stephen Rhinesmith's *Bring Home the World* is an excellent guide to the management of a volunteer community program.

Relations with foreign alumni

Some people argue that an institution's foreign student progam is incomplete unless it includes an organized effort to develop constructive ties with foreign alumni. Alumni abroad can seek out qualified students for an institution, screen applicants, help orient applicants who have been admitted, and help an institution's faculty members who might be traveling in their countries. They can find opportunities for collaborative research projects and help organize student exchanges.

Foreign alumni sometimes find each other to be welcome sources of social and professional support. They often appreciate being kept appraised of developments at the institutions from which they graduated, just as many American alumni do. In some cases, foreign alumni, like U.S. alumni, have made financial contributions to their alma maters.

FSA's who want to develop programs or services involving foreign alumni usually need to work with their alumni offices to determine what can be made available to alumni abroad and what contributions can reasonably be expected from them. Common impediments to the development of comprehensive foreign alumni programs are the difficulty of obtaining current addresses for them, the cost of international mail, the relatively low place foreign alumni usually hold in institutional priorities (and in the priorities of most alumni offices), and the amount of persistence and patience needed to get services and activities organized.

NAFSA's *Foreign Alumni: Overseas Links for U.S. Institutions* is a good starting point for FSA's who want to develop a foreign alumni program.

PROMOTING CULTURE LEARNING

Culture learning, at one level or another, is an integral part of foreign student advising. It involves acquiring knowledge of one or more other cultures, accepting culturally different people without judging them, and developing skill in interacting with people whose cultural backgrounds are different. FSA's often seek these goals concomitantly with their efforts to help foreign students adjust to American society and its academic system. Pre-arrival information, orientation programs, handbooks or other printed information, and individual advising are among the formats FSA's employ in this work with students from abroad.

While it seems clear that foreign students need to engage in at least a modicum of culture learning in order to cope with life in the United States, it is less clear, at least to some people, that the natives stand to gain something useful from interaction with culturally different people. Some people in the international educational exchange field argue that FSA's need not be concerned with culture learning among the host population because it is not relevant to their jobs. In my view, FSA's ought to be concerned with the hosts' attitudes toward and treatment of foreign students *for the sake of the foreign students*, if for no other reason. A receptive campus and community will make the foreign students' experience in the United States easier to manage and more beneficial.

FSA's, then, have a direct interest in culture learning among Americans. That interest is not widely acknowledged, though, so most FSA's face considerable frustration in their efforts to involve members of the host population in culture learning activities. There are other reasons, too, that account for the difficulties many FSA's confront when they organize culture learning programs or activities. Among them: FSA's do not usually have faculty status and so cannot usually offer grades or academic credit for teaching they might do; many people in the United States are simply not interested in culture learning and are not receptive to FSA's or anyone else who seems to be trying to tell them what is good for them and how they "should" improve; American students, staff and faculty and community members already have heavy demands on their time and energy and are not easily induced to give up some routine or clearly desirable part of their lives for the sake of something called "culture learning"; and it has not proven possible to measure the benefits of culture learning in a way that makes it attractive or desirable in the eyes of most U.S. students, faculty, staff, or community members.

Mestenhauser discusses other barriers to the success of a classroom culture learning activity that puts foreign students in the role of teacher. The barriers include "low level ethnocentrism" among the natives. His ideas, appearing in "Foreign Students as Teachers," are no doubt generalizable to other types of programs.

In the face of these obstacles, what can FSA's do to promote culture learning on their campuses and in their communities? They must begin with the characteristics of patience and perseverence. They have to develop skills in intercultural training (see Chapters Five and Six) or find someone who has them. Then begins the painstaking effort to find interested audiences and develop formats suitable for them.

Interested audiences might be found where there are problems in intercultural relationships, where something noteworthy and positive involving intercultural relationships has captured people's attention, or where there are people or organizations looking for a cause or an activity in which to invest themselves. Is there difficulty between foreign and American students in a residence hall, where staff members are looking for help in improving the situation? Or, on the contrary, has a group of students from abroad aroused other students' interest in learning about other cultures? Is there a student honorary or service club looking for a project? Or a community service or church group or parent-teacher organization in search of an activity in which to invest some effort?

There might be U.S. students preparing to go abroad or studying in a field where skill in intercultural relationships would be helpful.

There might be a staff committee looking for ideas for staff development activities. Maybe there is an academic department with a concentration of foreign students about whose educational and cultural backgrounds the faculty would like to learn more.

FSA's, if they look around carefully, can usually find some people who have an interest, at least an incipient one, in intercultural relationships. Some people might be interested in developing *awareness* or an improved *understanding* of cultural differences and their effects on people's behavior; others might be interested in learning *specific skills* that would enable them to engage in intercultural relations more constructively.

Finding formats suitable to these different audiences is a matter of considering how much time is available, what the audience's specific learning objectives are, their level of sophistication, the forms of instruction most likely to hold their attention, and the skills and materials FSA's or other trainers have at their disposal. In "Cross-Cultural Training," Peggy Pusch and her co-authors offer many useful ideas for the design of culture learning programs.

It seems to me that a mystique has developed around "cross-cultural training." The term conjures up the notion of highly trained specialists cleverly working with (some say "manipulating") an array of refined exercises to lead participants to some form of enlightenment. An oversimplified but more accurate image of the activity is this: intercultural learning begins when people with different cultural backgrounds begin to *talk* with each other. The trainer's job is to get the people together, provide an environment conducive to talk and a stimulus to conversation (an exercise, perhaps, or a film, or just a set of pertinent and interesting questions), and some help in overcoming culturally-based problems that interfere with the discussion. The latter might include assumptions and values that are not shared, differences in communicative style, or differences in patterns of thought.

Seen in this way, culture learning is something most FSA's can readily seek to promote, at least at the level of increasing awareness and understanding. Helping people develop *skills* in intercultural interaction may require some special knowledge and training.

Most recommended formats for cross-cultural learning programs call for the inclusion of foreign students in the activity. Panels, discussion groups, role plays, and intercultural workshops are clearly more effective in producing culture learning if they include participants from diverse cultures. FSA's who arrange culture learning programs will normally want to be sure that foreign students have a role in them.

At the same time, FSA's will want to avoid assuming that all foreign students are by definition interested in culture learning, either for themselves or for local students, staff, or community members. Some foreign students want to minimize their involvement with the local people. They do not want to share rooms with them, join them on picnics, show them dances from home, or join intercultural workshops. FSA's ought to respect these wishes, realizing that they may stem from a reasonable desire to be left alone or to minimize problems of re-entering their own societies.

ADMINISTRATION

Some FSA's have almost no administrative responsibilities. Others have many. Those who have many will want to look to other, more specialized publications than this one to learn about management techniques and administrative practices. This section offers a few general ideas that are intended to give some perspective to the administative aspect of foreign student advising.

The first requisite of efficient administration is to have clear objectives and well-established priorities. As was suggested in Chapter Six, FSA's will want to establish a routine for the periodic review of objectives and setting of priorities. The development of specific plans and budgets is contingent on this objective-setting.

Efficient administration also requires well-organized procedures for handling routine business. In a foreign student office, this might mean preparing printed handouts responding to the most frequently asked questions. Immigration procedures and routine institutional procedures lend themselves to this kind of treatment.

Having sheets for students to fill out when requesting immigration forms or enrollment certification letters also saves time. Instructions for the completion of routine forms can be posted.

We have already recommended providing written policy statements concerning financial aid and other arrangements for students in financial difficulty.

A foreign student office needs a good filing system. Papers in student files are often referred to again and again, so they need to be

filed promptly and accurately. Information on a wide array of topics needs to be retrievable. Some institutions are using automatic
data processing (ADP) for portions of their information storage and
FSA's will want to try to take advantage of these systems. There is
particular value in using ADP to retrieve statistical information
about the foreign student body—size, nationality and sex makeup,
fields of study, and so on. A "Guide for the Collection of Data on
Foreign Students" is available from NAFSA at the address given in
Appendix F.

In offices where there is noticeable personnel turnover, even if
only at the level of student assistants, it might be prudent to write an
office procedures manual for use in training and guiding employees.
Serious problems can develop when information about too many of
an office's procedures and policies is stored only in the head of one
mortal person.

Much of what happens in a foreign student office is routine, as
has been said, and clerical people can be taught to handle it. FSA's
will be doing themselves a favor if they train their clerical employees
to do as much routine work as possible, leaving themselves free to
work on longer-term projects. At institutions where the foreign students have been trained to believe they have to see the FSA personally about every single matter, the students can be retrained.

PROFESSIONAL DEVELOPMENT

It is probably clear from all that has gone before that FSA's have
to devote considerable attention to their own professional development if they want to do their jobs well.

The most accessible means of professional development is reading. The books and articles cited in this *Handbook* along with those
recommended in my *Learning Across Cultures* provide ample
suggestions.

Many educational institutions offer professional development
courses or sessions for their employees. These usually concern communication skills or management practices, training in both of
which can help FSA's. Participating in professional development
activities offered by one's own institution also provides opportunities
to extend contacts among colleagues.

Visits with FSA's at neighboring institutions can result in useful
information, new ideas about ways to handle particular problems,

suggestions for administrative improvements, plans or ideas for cooperative activities, and supportive, collegial relationships.

NAFSA publications and conferences have been mentioned repeatedly in this *Handbook*. In my view, membership in NAFSA and use of its publications is vital to responsible foreign student advising, not to mention professional development. One component of NAFSA, called the Field Service Program, is specifically concerned with the professional development of FSA's and others in the international educational exchange field. The Field Service Program offers a number of options for professional development, including in-service training grants to visit other institutions and learn from their personnel and programs and access to consultants who can be invited to one's own campus to review policies and procedures and make recommendations.

NAFSA conferences provide countless opportunities to acquire useful information, get a new perspective on one's work, and establish relationships with colleagues who can be helpful.

NAFSA's success depends on the volunteer efforts of hundreds of members who work on various committees, task forces, "teams" and specific projects. I have benefitted inestimably from active involvement in NAFSA, and I heartily recommend it to anyone who is willing to volunteer and then follow through on commitments. Knowledge, helpful acquaintances, and expanded opportunities for professional development will result. And fun, too, in the company of a remarkably interesting and concerned group of people.

From time to time FSA's can find seminars or workshops designed for foreign student advisers and perhaps others who work in intercultural situations. NAFSA periodically offers such programs, as do the organizations listed in Appendix M.

International travel is often considered the ideal form of professional development for foreign student advisers. My impression is that such travel can be quite beneficial, but is not necessarily so. Travel will help FSA's do their jobs better to the degree that it gives them the experience of being a foreigner, provides information about other cultures or educational systems, and acquaints them with the viewpoints of some people who see the world differently from the way they see it themselves.

Writing is another constructive approach to professional development. Writing an article, whether for a scholarly journal or the

NAFSA Newsletter or the local newspaper, requires research or other information-gathering along with systematic thought and reflection. Writing can help FSA's examine ideas or information they might otherwise overlook or consider only superficially.

Research projects on aspects of foreign student affairs are more than welcome if they are carefully done and well reported. In the eyes of many academics and high-level administrators, people in foreign student affairs are inadequately rigorous in their approach to their work. FSA's are often seen to lack basic data about foreign students—data about such things as enrollment trends, academic performance, the incidence of particular problems or issues, and many other matters. FSA's will do themselves credit if they routinely keep and analyze basic data about their clients. Beyond that, they can do and report on research projects on dozens and dozens of interesting topics relating to foreign students and intercultural relationships. See Spaulding & Flack's *The World's Students in the United States* and Lee, Abd-Ella, & Burk's *Needs of Foreign Students from Developing Nations at U.S. Colleges and Universities* for a lifetime supply of ideas for research topics.

Professional development for foreign student advisers does not require traveling abroad, going to conferences, or extensive reading. Conversations with foreign students can provide FSA's with an immense amount of useful information and insight. All that is needed is intelligent questions and respectful attention to answers. FSA's can learn useful things from foreign students virtually every working day.

Effective FSA's include professional development in their yearly plans. They identify topics they could benefit from knowing more about and make plans for learning about them. They allow time and allocate funds—if it is at all possible—for attending NAFSA or other conferences and meetings. They know they cannot stay abreast of developments in their complex and rapidly changing field unless they devote a significant amount of effort to professional development.

☞ 8

Conclusion

I sometimes remark to foreign students on the number of expressions in everyday American speech that come from baseball. Strike out, throw him a curve, out in left field, off the wall, touch base, batting one thousand—these and many other phrases come from a game that is unfamiliar in most parts of the world.

Stories from baseball (and other sports) are also quite common among Americans, and I want to tell one now. Maybe what I am about to relate did not really happen. I did not witness it. But if it did not happen, it could have.

The story is about Roberto Clemente, who played right field for the Pittsburgh Pirates from 1955 until his death in 1972. Among Pirate fans he was known as "The Great One." His lifetime batting average was an outstanding .317. Shortly before his death he got his three thousandth base hit, a feat accomplished by only twelve of the thousands of people who have played major league baseball in this country. Twelve times during his career he won the coveted Gold Glove Award for superior defensive play.

Clemente could hit and run and throw. I once saw him pick up a ball at the base of the right field fence and throw it all the way to the catcher—330 feet on the fly—to cut down a runner trying to score. He could catch balls that could not be caught and make throws that could not be made. He seemingly never got picked off a base and he almost never threw to the wrong place. When a ball bounced off the wall above him, he was always positioned to field it. He played with utter concentration and dedication, and he always tried to do better. He was awesome.

The story goes that a reporter asked him once why he worked so hard at playing the game of baseball. His reply: "I play this game the way it is supposed to be played."

This *Handbook* offers a great deal for foreign student advisers to think about and to do. Most FSA's will not undertake them all. I hope they will undertake as many as they can. Foreign student advising can not only be the most interesting job on the campus, but also a way to make a significant and constructive contribution toward solving what is in many ways the most fundamental problem of our age: people's inability to accept and work cooperatively with people who are different. The FSA's job, as Martin Limbird said, is to change the world. To do that requires dedication, concentration, and continuing effort to do better. That is the way the job is supposed to be done.

Do You Trust Your Foreign Student?

What constitutes "truth" and "honesty"? How important are these two values compared to others? Questions such as these commonly arise in theoretical discussions about intercultural communication. When they are faced in the real world, they are likely to be confounded, as they are in the case reported here, by the personal viewpoints and institutional responsibilities of the people involved. They become questions not just of theoretical interest, but of practical and ethical importance. Several questions are combined: What is "honesty"? How does one determine who is being honest? How important is honesty in a given situation? Who has the strongest claim to the loyalty of an educational institution's staff members who are hired to work with students from other countries? All these issues arose in the case reported here.

The last time Mehrdad (fictional name, as are the others in this account) came to the Foreign Student Office to apply for financial aid, he was in the final semester of his senior year. He did not have money for his semester's tuition or for all of his living expenses. All he had, according to his application form, was a few hundred dollars—proceeds from the sale of some furniture and some books, and from a summer job. "I owe the completion of my education entirely to you," he wrote to the Foreign Student Aid Committee. "I will appreciate any financial assistance you might be able to give me."

The Foreign Student Aid Committee did have some money available for allocation to foreign students who demonstrated their financial need. When it had money for helping foreign students in

Note: This article originally appeared under a different title in *Intercultural Theory and Practice: A Case Method Approach*, edited by William Davey. It is reprinted here with the

need, the Foreign Student Aid Committee allocated it periodically after reviewing applications submitted to the Foreign Student Office. The aid was formally allocated by a subcommittee of the Foreign Student Aid Committee, and that subcommittee was often composed only of the two foreign student advisers (FSA's) who worked in the Foreign Student Office. On occasion, at the request of the FSA's, faculty members of the Foreign Student Aid Committee participated in the evaluation of applications for financial aid. Mehrdad had applied for and received financial aid through the Foreign Student Aid Committee on two previous occasions, and had on one other occasion sought the Foreign Student Office's assistance in getting financial aid through the Student Financial Aid Office, which assisted foreign students only on rare occasions.

Thus, when Mehrdad sought financial aid during his final semester, there had been a long history of interaction among him, the Foreign Student Office, and the Foreign Student Aid Committee. The history of Mehrdad's involvement with these offices, and indeed of his entire stay at the University, needs to be recounted to put the events surrounding his final application into perspective.

From the point of view of the Foreign Student Office, Mehrdad's relationship to The University began as relationships with Iranian students very often did—with a visit from a relative. In this case, Mehrdad's brother Mozafar visited the Foreign Student Office in the summer of 1975 to make sure that Mehrdad's application for admission was progressing through channels as expeditiously as possible. The application had been submitted to the Admissions Office only one day before Mozafar's visit. Mozafar was less than pleased to learn that even his calling personally on the Foreign Student Office could not make the application pass through three different offices in the course of one day. Mozafar was himself a graduate of The University, having compiled an above-average academic record in the College of Horticulture, and he had hoped his standing *vis-a-vis* The University would hasten the processing of his brother Mehrdad's application.

Mehrdad's application was approved in due course. His dossier showed that he had earned an A.S. degree at The Community College nearby. He had a grade point average of 3.5 The FSA

permission of the Society for Intercultural Education, Training, and Research, 1414 Twenty-second Street, N.W., Washington, D.C. 20037.

at The Community College had written on Mehrdad's behalf: "I recommend him as a very capable student." The financial documents accompanying his application said he would receive $400 monthly from his father in Iran, and that his brother Mozafar agreed to meet all of Mehrdad's financial needs during his first year at The University. Mozafar was a permanent resident of the U.S., living with his American wife in the town where The Community College was located. So Mehrdad began his studies in the College of Horticulture in August, 1975. He registered for 19 semester hours, a heavier than average course load. He finished the semester registered for 15 hours, and had a g.p.a. of 2.0. His grades included one F and one D.

The following March 13, Mozafar and Mehrdad appeared together at the Foreign Student Office. They wanted a Form I-20 for Mehrdad, who was planning a trip home. (A Form I-20 is an immigration form needed, in a case like this, to re-enter the United States.) They also wanted a letter certifying that Mehrdad was a full-time student. But a check with the registrar disclosed that Mehrdad was not a full-time student. His registration had been cancelled the previous week. The cancellation was necessitated, Mehrdad said, by his hospitalization for an appendectomy and the subsequent period of convalescence. Mehrdad had missed so many classes that he could not possibly do well academically during the semester, so he had cancelled his registration. He had been a full-time student until he cancelled, Mehrdad and Mozafar argued, and his cancellation was due to circumstances beyond his control. So it was reasonable to state in a letter that he was a full-time student, they maintained.

The FSA was suspicious, feeling that he was being pressured. Why had they both come with this routine request? Why were they so vehement? With the brothers waiting outside, the FSA telephoned the business office of the hospital where the appendectomy allegedly took place. There was no record that Mehrdad had ever been a patient there. The FSA tried to telephone the surgeon who had allegedly performed the appendectomy, but he had moved to another hospital. The hospital was known, however, for misplacing records, so the FSA was unwilling to conclude that Mehrdad was lying. Back in the FSA's office, aware that he was being regarded skeptically, Mehrdad asked, "Do you want to see my scar?" "No," said the FSA, "I'll believe what you say."

The FSA gave Mehrdad the I-20, because there was no indication that he could not re-enroll at The University. The FSA also prepared a letter stating that Mehrdad had been a full-time student until March 8, when medical problems had compelled him to cancel his registration.

In September, the Foreign Student Office received a copy of a letter in which the Admissions Office informed Mehrdad that he had been admitted to the College of Cartography. This seemingly routine letter was filed by a secretary and was not brought to the attention of the FSA. Later in September, Mehrdad presented the Foreign Student Office with the first of his applications for financial aid from the Foreign Student Aid Committee. On the application Mehrdad had written that his father had become ill and had had to use money intended for Mehrdad's education for his own medical expenses. Besides, his father had five other children to put through school. Mehrdad said his need amounted to more than $4000 and that the Foreign Student Aid Committee was "the only place" he could get any financial help. He came personally to the Foreign Student Office almost once daily to find out what action had been taken on his application, and was told each time that he would hear from the Committee in writing as soon as a decision on his application was reached.

Because aid from the Foreign Student Aid Committee cannot exceed the amount of a student's tuition (a fact clearly stated on the application form) and Mehrdad's tuition amounted to only $1560 for the year, the Foreign Student Aid Committee wrote to him and said it could not help him. It said he needed more than he could possibly get from the Foreign Student Aid Committee and if in fact the Foreign Student Aid Committee was his "only place" to get assistance, there was no point in trying to aid him.

Mehrdad replied to the Committee in writing, saying that he had talked to his brother, who had agreed to pay his rent and help him buy food. He said that he had applied to his government for aid and that he was looking, so far unsuccessfully, for a job.

The Foreign Student Aid Committee, through its subcommittee, allocated him $500 for the fall semester, 1976.

In January 1977 he applied for $916 in aid, citing the same reasons he had previously given to account for his financial hardship. Again he visited the Foreign Student Office almost daily to inquire about his application. He was allocated $275, an amount substantially less than his tuition for the semester. In February, he wrote to the Foreign Student Aid Committee saying "I am a senior and need only 9 more hours to graduate." He was registered for 25 semester hours, and faced cancellation of his registration if he did not pay the remainder of his tuition. By this time the Foreign Student Aid Committee had no more money to allocate. The FSA, thinking that he and The University were nearly rid of what had come to seem a real problem, appealed to the Student Financial Aid Office to assist Mehrdad in paying tuition for what he said was his final semester. The Student Financial Aid Office complied and allocated $518 to Mehrdad.

Meanwhile, elsewhere, other events that came to have a bearing on this case were taking place. An Iranian graduate of The University began courting a female staff member at The University. He presented himself as an employee of his government, with responsibilities that made it necessary for him to travel frequently between Iran and the U.S. He said he often visited the town where The University was located, because he had friends there. He provided expensive entertainment for the lady and bought her gifts. He showed her photographs of his home in Tehran and was not careful to hide the large amounts of cash he had in his wallet.

A few weeks later, about the middle of March, it emerged that the "government employee" was not what he presented himself to be, in his elaborate stories about his work, his family members in Tehran, events taking place in various airports, and conversations held during trans-Atlantic flights. The man was in fact Mehrdad's brother, Mozafar, who still lived in the nearby town where The Community College was located. He was stepping out on his wife and spending a large amount of money on the lady who worked at The University.

This activity of Mozafar's became known to at least two members of the Foreign Student Aid Committee, although it was never openly discussed. "There's no financial need in that family," one Foreign Student Aid Committee member declared, without explaining where his understanding of the family's financial situation had come from. Said another Foreign Student Aid Committee member: "No one in that family is ever going to get anything from The University if I have anything to do with it."

Late the following August, Mehrdad appeared again at the Foreign Student Office and submitted another application for financial aid from the Foreign Student Aid Committee. He asked for more than $1000. He said he had taken loans from friends totalling $1750, and had a medical bill of $60 that he could not pay. He was registered for 20 semester hours of class, and he said in an accompanying letter to the Foreign Student Aid Committee that he would graduate at the end of the semester. "I owe the completion of my education entirely to you," he wrote.

As in the past, Mehrdad paid daily calls on the Foreign Student Office to ask whether there had been a decision on his application. As in the past he was told each time that the Committee had not met yet, and that he would be informed of its decision as soon as one was made.

In early September the Foreign Student Aid Committee wrote him in response to his application. They pointed out that he had told them during the previous semester that he would graduate in the summer, and they wanted to know why he was still at The University and had not graduated. They asked about his previously-mentioned application for financial aid from his government, which he had said he submitted 11 months earlier. They referred to his brother's earlier commitment of financial support, and asked to see a written statement from the brother affirming that he could not or would not support Mehrdad. Some members of the Foreign Student Aid Committee, it should be remembered, were convinced that Mehrdad's brother Mozafar, who lived only 40 miles away, possessed large amounts of money.

Mehrdad replied in writing the following day. He said he would have graduated at the end of the summer session if he had been able to afford to attend the summer session, but he had not had the money, and so had worked instead. He said he had not had a response to his inquiry to his government, and that his brother Mozafar was in debt and could not pay more for Mehrdad's education.

The following day a letter came from Mozafar declaring that he was $10,000 in debt and could not support Mehrdad. A few days after that, Mozafar, who had shown a pile of currency to that lady he was courting, appeared at the Foreign Student Office and showed an FSA documents reflecting debts totalling about $10,000. They included loans from various banks, amounts due to two different credit card companies and to some local merchants, and $1,000 due The University for an educational loan.

Perplexed, the FSA made some phone calls to faculty members who had reason to be acquainted with Mehrdad. First, the Administrative Director of the College of Horticulture, where Mehrdad was first enrolled when he came to The University. Mehrdad had been accused of cheating while in the College of Horticulture, the Administrative Director said, and had been given the option of cancelling his registration rather than facing formal proceedings. He had cancelled with the understanding that he would never again be allowed to be a candidate for a Horticulture degree. This had happened in March, 1976, at the time of the alleged appendectomy. The charges of cheating "absolutely could be proven," the Administrative Director said.

The Administrative Director went on to note that, despite the fact the Mehrdad had been told he could never earn a degree from the College of Horticulture, he was continuing to enroll in classes there. And he was signing up for many "independent study" courses in the College, thereby, according to the Administrative Director, avoiding the heavier work he would have to do if he were in regular classes.

Next, the FSA talked with the Professor of Old Maps, Mehrdad's current adviser in the College of Cartography, to which Mehrdad had transferred after leaving the College of Horticulture. The Professor said Mehrdad could indeed have graduated the previous summer if he had taken the right courses, but he kept dropping and adding more courses to get more Horticulture courses on his record. He did not seem to be trying to graduate in Cartography. "I don't know who signs all his drop-add slips," the Professor of Old Maps said, "Maybe he signs them himself." He went on, "I would recommend that no financial aid be given to him."

The FSA reviewed Mehrdad's permanent record. It did indeed reflect some courses being dropped and others added, but the changes did not result in a net decrease in the number of his Cartography courses. The Professor of Old Maps had been wrong about that. And the FSA asked an official in the registrar's office to look at Mehrdad's drop-add slips to see if they appeared to have been signed by a single person. Not at all, came the report. The Professor's suggestion that Mehrdad was manipulating his courses in an unauthorized way did not appear to be well-founded.

The FSA talked with the Administrative Director of the College of Cartography. The Adminstrative Director was blunt: "I'd vote against aid. Mehrdad was caught cheating in three different classes here. I don't think he needs the money either." This Administrative Director happened to be a member of the Foreign Student Aid Committee.

The FSA checked with the Transcript Analyst and asked if Mehrdad could have graduated the previous May or July. Yes, he could have, came the report, if he had not dropped two courses during the previous semester.

Five members of the Foreign Student Aid Committee met on September 16 to discuss Mehrdad's application. They voted not to allocate him anything and sent him a letter saying that he would receive no aid because he could have graduated the previous semester.

The day he received the letter, Mehrdad went to the Foreign Student Office. He was with an FSA for about an hour and one-half. He made several points, each repeatedly and with emphasis. He said the Professor of Old Maps had misled him the previous semester when he told him he could graduate at the end of that semester, because the Professor of Old Maps had been unaware that all of Mehrdad's credits from The Community College could not be counted toward his degree from The University. Mehrdad said he could not have taken all the Cartography courses he needed during the previous semester because they were not all offered and because some were prerequisites for others.

He said he had not cheated while in the College of Horticulture. "They never proved I cheated," he said. "Look at my grades from The Community College and from my high school. They are good grades. Does the Administrative Director think I cheated to get all those grades?"

"And even if I did cheat, that is not the Foreign Student Aid Committee's business. The Foreign Student Aid Committee is supposed to decide if I need money, not if I cheated.

"I did not withdraw from all those courses myself last semester. The Administrative Director of Horticulture withdrew me from them and put me into other ones. Those were independent study courses. Look at my transcript. You can see that there are withdrawals from higher level courses that have been replaced on my record with lower level courses. I didn't do that. The Administrative Director did that. He never said any word to me about it."

And he talked about his brother. He said he knew his brother had dated that University employee and tried to make a big impression by spending a lot of money on her. "That is a problem with my brother and not with me," he said. "I have my own financial problems. I want to graduate. I am not responsible for my brother's morals."

Mehrdad was in tears. "I am desperate," he said. "I want to graduate. I am already in debt. I have no money. My brother is in debt and he cannot help me."

The FSA was noncommital. "The main issue as far as the Foreign Student Aid Committee is concerned is whether you could have graduated by now," he said. "You told the Committee last year that you would be graduated by now, but you are still here. You are saying now that you were operating on the basis of bad information from the Professor of Old Maps when you made that statement. I will have to discuss this with the Professor of Old Maps."

The Professor was out of town when the FSA called. He returned the FSA's call eleven days later. Yes, the Professor said, he had been confused about how much of Mehrdad's Community College credit would apply toward a degree from The University. Mehrdad probably could not have graduated any earlier.

The two FSA's consulted and agreed to allocate $570 to Mehrdad from the Foreign Student Aid Committee fund. This was less than Mehrdad needed to pay his tuition, so an FSA urged the Student Financial Aid Office to loan Mehrdad the balance of his tuition, to be repaid following his long-awaited graduation. The loan was made, and never repaid.

"Foreign" vs. "International": Can "International Man" Be Stopped?

A number of important debates or discussions are going on in international education circles these days. They involve such topics as special tuition rates for foreign students (in the U.S. and abroad), the relevance of curricula for students from other countries, and the role of the United States Immigration and Naturalization Service in educational exchange. There is another topic of controversy that remains lively in personal conversations, but has not found its way into the media. That is the question of whether students in the U.S. from other countries should be called "foreign students" or "international students." This brief essay concerns that topic, which, while mundane in comparison to the topics mentioned above, appears to excite the emotions of many who debate it.

For many years, the term "foreign students" was widely used and accepted to refer to students in the U.S. from other countries. Then, like certain other common phrases in the vocabulary of people concerned with international affairs, for example, "underdeveloped country" and "illegal alien," it was challenged by people who thought it was somehow improper, and the term "international students" began to take its place.

The new term has been and continues to be resisted by people who thought it entailed a loss of meaning or precision. The argument in favor of "international students" is typically this: "Some people think the word 'foreign' has a negative connotation, so we shouldn't use it. The word 'international' does not have that connotation, so it is better."

Note: This article originally appeared in the *NAFSA Newsletter* for April, 1980.

It is interesting to notice that this argument almost always refers to *someone else* who allegedly ascribes the negative connotation to "foreign." One virtually never hears anyone say, "I think the word 'foreign' has a negative connotation."

What does the term "international students" have in its favor, besides the putative blessing of unnamed other people who allegedly think "foreign" sounds unpleasant? Very little, it seems. And there is no doubt that, like many euphemisms, it is far less precise than the term it was intended to replace.

Just what is an "international student"? A fruitful way to explore that question begins with consideration of the label applied to Volkswagons and Datsuns in the U.S. These vehicles are called "foreign cars." Everyone agrees that a "foreign car" is a car manufactured in one country and now being used in another. That is, the term evokes a common meaning and has no particular negative connotation.

What would an "international car" be? A number of possibilities come to mind. It could be a car made of parts that were manufactured in more than one country, and/or assembled by workers of diverse nationalities. It could be a car that belonged to an international organization, or one that frequently crossed a boundary between two countries. It could also be a car that was built in one country and was being used in another, although it would be stretching things to derive that meaning from "international car."

Following this line of thought, let us explore the possible meanings of "international student." The term might refer to a student at the United Nations University, or one who frequently crossed a national boundary to go to school, or one whose area of study was international affairs. It could be a student whose parents were of different nationalities.

It could be a student who was conceived or born aboard a ship in international waters or aboard an aircraft in international airspace. And, of course, it could be a student who was born in one country and is now studying in another, although it would be stretching things to derive that meaning from "international student."

Despite its lack of clarity, "international student" has attained wide usage. And, to the chagrin of people who admire precision in the use of language, the notion that "international" is an appropriate adjective for referring to foreigners is spreading. We are now hearing the term "international women" with increasing frequency.

It is apparently supposed to refer to female foreign students and to foreign wives of visiting scholars. That is, it apparently refers to what could be called, with admirable precision, "foreign women."

So far, we have been spared "international man," but the way things are going that grotesquerie is probably almost upon us. Unless, perhaps, there is concerted action on the part of those who still believe that careful use of language is worth defending. People of that persuasion, derisively called "purists" by those who readily support any change in usage as a welcome example of adaptability, seem to have few effective weapons against the onslaught of new and vague terms. They have unsuccessfully opposed many recent additions to the vocabulary of the educational world, including "interface," "thrust" (as a noun), and "impact" (as a verb). Can "international man" be stopped? Could we even roll back to "foreign student"? Good-natured ridicule may be the best weapon in the hands of the purists. "There's an international man who wants you on the phone," we might say to one of those people who knows someone who allegedly thinks "foreign" has a negative connotation. "There are two international men waiting to see you." And so on. In this way purists might be able to make their meaning clear.

APPENDIX **C**

The D.I.E. Formulation

Explain to a group of participants in an orientation program or other session about intercultural relations that the purpose of the D.I.E formulation is to illuminate three different aspects of people's response to intercultural (and other human) interactions. Write on the blackboard:

D

I

E

Then explicate, on the board:

Describe—what you *see*

Interpret—what you *think* about what you see

Evaluate—what you *feel* about what you see

Get an example of something someone has said about some human behavior in an intercultural situation. An example that emerged in a session I recently conducted came from a Malaysian student whom I had asked to tell about the first class she attended in the United States. "It was chaotic" when she went into the classroom, the student said. "The students were very unruly and very disrespectful of the teacher."

I pointed out that this "description," like many people's descriptions of things they see other people do, was not just a description, but a combination of interpretation ("the students were very disrespectful") and evaluation ("chaotic, unruly"). I explained that this "description" told me nothing about what was happening in the classroom. It told me only what the student thought and felt about it. That might be relevant in some way, but it was not what I wanted. After all, I would no doubt have my own thoughts and feelings about the classroom situation, and they would inevitably be different from the student's, since we are different people with different standards. I explained that the classroom situation could be described in terms of the number of students in the room, their positions and postures, the number who were talking, the volume of their voices, the other activities in which they were participating (drinking coffee, reading the student newspaper, and so on). This would be a Description. Anyone seeing the classroom could see the same things. No Interpretation or Evaluation is involved. Interpretation is subjective, Evaluation more so. People in intercultural situations will inevitably misinterpret some (or much) of what they see, and their evaluations will inevitably be based on standards inappropriate to the new culture. People in intercultural situations, including foreign students and foreign student advisers, ought therefore to learn to distinguish Description from Interpretation from Evaluation, and then to try, relentlessly, to stop Evaluating.

The Intercultural Meeting

A common source of frustration for administrators of foreign student programs is the "international student club," or whatever the local organization of foreign (and sometimes U.S.) students is called. "We sent out a notice about an organizational meeting," an FSA might report, "and a reasonable number of students showed up. But the meeting went on and on and got nowhere." Or, "We have an international student club, but it doesn't do much. The meetings are exercises in frustration."

From the viewpoint of the adviser who believes it would be salutary to have an active international student club on a campus, it is usually the club's meetings that are the focus of the greatest discontent. The meetings tend to be long, unproductive, and often disputatious. Why should this be? A look at people's culturally-based ideas about meetings might suggest some answers to that question. Before looking at those ideas, though, it is important to mention other possible explanations for the problems advisers face in fostering the development of international student clubs. These have to do with the adviser's and students' discrepant assumptions concerning such clubs.

An adviser who decides to call an organizational meeting for an international student club is probably making most, if not all, of the following assumptions:

— It would be constructive to have an international student club, to foster interaction between foreign and U.S. students and/or to provide social activities for foreign students.

Note: This article originally appeared in the *NAFSA Newsletter* for November, 1981.

— It is possible to have an international student club that is divorced from the political interests and viewpoints of the students.

— Students view the staff of the foreign student office as benevolent, apolitical, and capable of organizing situations that benefit most foreign students.

— Students from diverse countries see themselves as having important interests in common. They will be able to agree upon objectives for an organization and will willingly cooperate with each other in seeking those objectives.

All of these assumptions are open to question. But even if they are all accurate, and the international student club gets to the point where meetings are held, the problems are only beginning. People with differing cultural backgrounds bring such diverse assumptions and behaviors to meetings that their gatherings are often rife with misunderstandings.

In *Beyond Culture*, anthropologist Edward Hall offers the notion of "action chains." An action chain is a series of behaviors which people who grow up in a particular culture are taught (usually implicitly) to view as appropriate for a particular situation. People follow their action chains without having to think about what they are doing, or why they are doing it. The situation evokes the behavior.

One situation that evokes certain behaviors is a "meeting." What does the concept of meeting mean to people of different cultures? What behavior is appropriate at a meeting?

To Americans, it seems quite sensible to summon interested people to an organizational meeting for an international student club. It is assumed that interested people will appear at the appointed time and place. There will be a leader, probably elected in some way, or appointed for a temporary period by someone in authority. The leader will moderate the discussion, recognizing people who wish to speak, summarizing people's comments and keeping speakers on the track.

There will be discussion at the meeting. Everyone who wants to talk will have an opportunity to do so. People attending the meeting will seek a common ground (that is, they will compromise), establishing a foundation for subsequent joint action. Agreements will be ratified, probably by means of a vote. If the group is large or the issue complicated, Robert's Rules of Order will be employed to manage the discussion. Otherwise, informality will prevail.

Not everyone has this same action chain concerning meetings. There can be diverse assumptions about several aspects of meetings: why they are held, the means of selecting a leader, the leader's role, and the role and behavior of those attending the meeting. Some of the various assumptions that people from different cultures make about these topics are discussed here.

WHY MEETINGS ARE HELD

Americans typically hold meetings in order to share information or to make decisions. People from elsewhere might, more often than Americans, hold meetings in order to ratify or formalize decisions that are made elsewhere, or to give people an opportunity to air their views in the absence of an intention to make any decisions. Of course, people who go to a meeting with the assumption that some decisions are to be made will be frustrated if there are others there who are at the meeting merely to express their opinions.

MEANS OF SELECTING A LEADER

Most people make the assumption that a meeting needs a leader, although there are people who do not assume that. Among those who do suppose there should be a leader, there are diverse views about the means by which the leader should be designated. In some cultures, a person's age and/or social standing would automatically make him or her the leader in the eyes of all those present. In other cultures a formal nomination and election procedure would be employed. Other possibilities for selecting a leader include having someone volunteer to be the leader, waiting for a leader to emerge from the proceedings, or having the leader appointed by someone in authority.

At a meeting of students from different countries, especially one held for the purpose of organizing an international student club, these diverse ideas about leadership selection are likely to cause problems. A leader chosen by some people's method may not have legitimacy in the eyes of others. In fact, the others might not even realize that some of the people at the meeting believe a leader has been recognized.

THE LEADER'S ROLE

Americans typically suppose that a leader who is acting appropriately in the context of a meeting will serve as a moderator—keeping order, calling on speakers, preventing anyone from dominating the proceedings, assuring that everyone who wishes to speak has the opportunity to do so, keeping people's remarks on the subject, and helping the group reach decisions. It is often expected that the leader will be neutral with respect to topics of disagreement that arise during the meeting.

In many other societies, the leader is expected to exercise much more authority, and even to make important decisions on behalf of the group. In the eyes of people from such societies, the "democratic" style of group leadership that Americans tend to idealize is likely to seem unsatisfactory. It may give members so much opportunity to present diverse comments that the result seems like chaos. Or the leader's presumably greater wisdom may be seen as getting too little attention.

On the other hand, in societies where it is the norm to reach decisions by consensus, a U.S.-style chairman might seem too obtrusive.

ROLE AND BEHAVIOR OF MEETING PARTICIPANTS

It is probably the culturally influenced differences in group members' action chains for meetings that account for most of the difficulty at international student club meetings. First, there is the question of the role of people who attend meetings. In general, when a person comes to a meeting, he or she makes some assessment of his or her status in the group, because one's status within the group does much to determine how one is supposed to behave during the meeting. Determining one's status in a meeting of students from diverse countries is essentially impossible because there is no agreed-upon criterion or set of criteria for deciding where group members stand *vis-a-vis* each other. Possible criteria include age, sex, period of time as a student at the school, previous leadership position within the group, being from a rich or large country, being from the country or region with the largest number of foreign students at the particular school, being an officer in a nationality organization at the school, having a charismatic personality, or having some special affiliation with the foreign student office.

With all of these (and no doubt other) criteria being used by different people at the meeting to determine how they fit in, and with these determinations being made in the absence of conscious thought, discrepant conclusions are inevitable. Some people at the meeting will think that others are out of line.

Second, there is not likely to be a shared assumption about the overall function of the meeting. For Americans, as has been said, the unspoken assumption is that people at a meeting will "give and take" to reach compromise agreements that serve as the basis for action. For many others, though, compromise is not seen as natural or desirable. And there is less of an orientation to action. The purpose of the meeting may be to win all arguments, or at least to block the progress of those with opposing views or to display one's rhetorical talent. Engaging in what Americans are likely to consider "mere talk" may be, according to some people's assumptions, the basic function of the meeting. People who behave according to these assumptions often seem dogmatic, insensitive and obstructionist in the eyes of those who want to find compromises and make decisions.

A third source of disharmony in meetings of foreign students is differences in what Dean Barnlund calls "communicative style." (See *Public and Private Self in Japan and the United States.*) Only two aspects of communicative style will be discussed here. They are the general manner of interaction in a discussion, and the means by which people reach conclusions in their arguments.

Americans generally prefer a style of interaction that Barnlund labels "repartee." According to that style, no one speaks for very long. A speaker gets to the point quickly, then gives way to another speaker. A person who talks for too long gets a disapproving reaction.

A style prevalent in many other societies encourages much longer presentations from each speaker. Students from those societies are likely to view American-style presentations as superficial and perhaps lacking in rhetorical skill.

Meetings of foreign students nearly always include some students who, from the viewpoint of others who are present, talk too long. Impatience results.

People from different cultures are likely to manifest different ways of presenting their arguments. In a meeting of foreign students, one student's logic is likely to be another's nonsense. Some speakers will cite what they consider to be objective evidence to support their views. Others will invoke authorities of some kind. Others will make appeals to sentiment or emotion. Still others will endorse philosophical principles they wish the group to follow.

With two or more different ways of arguing in use at once, failures to understand are inevitable. Impatience and frustration result.

Given all the difficulties confronting an intercultural meeting, it is little wonder that international student clubs are so often dominated by one energetic leader and his or her compatriots. They have the same action chain for meetings.

There are things advisers can do to make intercultural meetings more productive. At a minimum they can foster learning about cultural differences. If the students attending the meeting can be helped to understand the ideas that appear in this article, they will have learned a good deal about themselves, about other cultures, about the influence of culture on their own and other people's behavior, and about the difficulties that beset intercultural encounters. They might be able to work together to surmount those difficulties.

Advisers could use various approaches to helping students learn from the cultural differences that are manifest in intercultural meetings. They could attend the international student club's meetings and offer observations about culturally based behavior they see taking place there. They could have students from a particular country describe for others their action chain for meetings. Better yet, students from particular countries could conduct brief mock meetings that other students could observe, and then there could be discussion of what has been seen. Such an exercise could sharpen students' ability to observe and analyze manifestations of cultural differences.

Another possibility is to have students from a particular country describe and show how they customarily conduct meetings, and then have all students use that action chain for the meeting. Different groups' action chains could be used at different meetings.

Still another possibility is to have the club's leader explain his or her conception of the leader's role and his or her expectations of group members. Making these conceptions and expectations explicit can reduce the amount of frustration and anger that result from behavior that others do not understand.

A relatively common approach to the problem of unsatisfactory international student clubs is to try to teach the students the idealized American action chain for meetings. This often takes the name of "leadership training" or "organizational behavior consulting." Such training is best accompanied by explicit acknowledgment of the U.S. cultural assumptions and values on which it is based.

Given all the cultural differences that are manifest in meetings of international student clubs, it is to be expected that such meetings will be unsatisfying for many of the people who attend them. If they are used as occasions for learning about cultural differences, they can be made more productive. If those in attendance are able to find ways to overcome the difficulties that their diverse cultural backgrounds cause them, some very important lessons will have been learned.

Foreign Students and Double Standards

Concern is often expressed in the academic community that double standards not be applied in the grading of foreign and U.S. students. It is said to be unfair to U.S. students if foreign students are not held to the same standards as U.S. students when grades are being determined.

There are many respects, though, in which foreign students are commonly expected to meet *higher* standards than U.S. students are. The result of this is unfairness to foreign students, who, when these double standards are applied, do not receive the sympathy, assistance, or even simple understanding that is accorded U.S. students.

Below are examples of a number of areas in which foreign students are often held to higher standards than U.S. students. Not everyone in the academic community holds to double standards in all the areas mentioned here, of course, but it is not difficult to find college and university faculty and staff members who adhere to one or more of these ideas.

—*Foreign students are supposed to do well academically.* It is assumed that U.S. students will represent the complete range of academic aptitude and performance, from excellent to unacceptable. College and university personnel may not be pleased when U.S. students settle for the "gentlemanly 'C,'" but they understand it and accept it. For foreign students, though, a mediocre performance is less acceptable. Foreign students are supposed to be good

---

Note: This article originally appeared under a slightly different title in the *NAFSA News-letter* for November, 1978.

students, and those who do poorly are likely to be considered as products of mistakes by the admissions committee rather than as parts of the normal range of student performance.

—*Foreign students are supposed to master English.* U.S. students often use the English language with less grace or facility than their teachers desire, and that fact is often deplored. But it is more or less understood and accepted. Whether it is attributed to a poor family environment, bad secondary schools and/or television, U.S. students' poor English is seen as the product of understandable forces over which the student had no particular control. But when foreign students do not use colloquial English with relative ease, they are often blamed for it as individuals. The fact that they did not even speak English at home is overlooked. So is the fact that English is taught in many of the world's secondary schools with methods even less successful than the methods used to teach foreign languages in the U.S. Also overlooked is the fact that the student's opportunities to practice English have been limited. The foreign student who does not use English with relative ease is often viewed as a person with a defective intellect, not as one who has suffered from a lack of opportunity to study and practice the language.

—*Foreign students are supposed to have enough money.* It is well known that the cost of attending U.S. post-secondary schools has risen rapidly in recent years. Because of this it is easily understood and accepted when U.S. students inquire about financial aid or seek part-time work. They have no choice; money is scarce and expenses are high. Besides, it is good to see them showing the drive and determination needed to succeed under adverse circumstances.

But foreign students are supposed to have enough money. Even though most of them come from countries far less well off than the U.S., they are often received with annoyance rather than with understanding when they inquire about financial aid or the possibilities for part-time work at U.S. educational institutions.

—*Foreign students are supposed to behave well.* Although the phrase "boys will be boys" is now impolitic and thus not so often heard these days, it still conveys the accepted notion that young people, especially males, will naturally exhibit unruly behavior from time to time. North American boys, that is. Foreign students are supposed to behave well. They are, after all, representatives of their countries. They are supposed to try at all times to make a good impression, to be polite, complimentary, and grateful, and to avoid doing things that might sully the image of "foreign students" in general.

—*Foreign students are supposed to be honest.* U.S. students are expected to dissemble from time to time, whether the purpose is to avoid appearing incompetent, reduce the amount of blame they may receive, or simply to get the best deal for themselves in a particular situation. These are all normal motives, and people who work with U.S. students know that it is frequently necessary to question them closely and perhaps seek corroboration from others before acting on what the students themselves have to say.

But foreign students are supposed to be honest. Whatever the cost in self-esteem or in other interests, foreign students are expected to tell the truth, the whole truth and nothing but the truth. If they do not, they tend to be be viewed as devious and untrustworthy.

—*Foreign students are expected to be quiet politically.* U.S. students are told of the virtues of free speech and assembly and are encouraged to become informed, active citizens. They are urged to get information about the issues, contemplate that information, and then take stands. Not so foreign students. Quiet speeches on political topics might be acceptable, but nothing more dramatic than that. The best foreign students, in this context, exhibit the kind of behavior that is condemned as "apathy" among their U.S. counterparts— they go to class, do their studies, and show no interest in contemporary political issues.

—*Foreign students are supposed to be chaste.* It is accepted as natural for young U.S. students to seek outlets for their sexual energies and interests. That is part of growing up. Only the more flagrant displays of sexual activity on the part of U.S. students will draw particular attention and condemnation.

Foreign students, though, are supposed to be chaste. Somehow it is just not right for them to seek outlets for their sexual energies and interests. Unless, perhaps, they confine their activities to members of their own nationality groups.

—*Foreign students are not supposed to have personal problems.* It is accepted that any group of U.S. students will normally include people who are having personal difficulties of some kind. The difficulties may involve loneliness, trouble in relating to others, making an occupational choice, problems with a romance, or some other concern. Whatever the problem, it is accepted as something that happens in the natural course of events. Some in the academic community may choose to try to help students having these problems, while others may prefer not to get involved, but few people condemn the student who is having the difficulty.

But foreign students are not supposed to have personal problems. They just shouldn't. It is too inconvenient, and there is no ready place to get help for them. The foreign student with personal problems, unlike his U.S. counterparts, is likely to be regarded as a person with a defective mind or character, someone who probably ought to leave school, go back home, and stop bothering people here.

—*Foreign students are supposed to live in a particular place after graduation.* U.S. students are expected to go wherever adventure or opportunity leads them after they graduate, to learn more about the world or to earn the best living they can. Foreign students, though, are supposed to go "home." If they do not, there is something vaguely dishonorable about them.

—*Foreign students are expected to do certain kinds of work after graduation.* U.S. students are expected to do whatever kind of work they enjoy, if they can find it, or whatever work is available if they cannot find something they enjoy. There is no general supposition that they should undertake any particular kind of activity. But foreign students, after they get "home," are supposed to do work that will help their countries "develop." They have that obligation, according to the common conception. Also, according to that common conception, the U.S. is "developed," the foreign student's country is not, and the foreign student has learned any number of things in the U.S. that, when skillfully applied at home, will make home more like the U.S.

Perhaps some of these examples have been overdrawn. The point is that it is easy to find within the U.S. academic commmunity (and in the community at large) people who apply a higher set of standards when judging foreign students than they use when judging domestic students. It is not difficult to understand why this is so. At least four things help account for it. First, for a long time the students who came to the U.S. from abroad were unusually well-educated, highly motivated, mature, sophisticated individuals. They did good academic work, behaved well, and so on. There are many people still active in the U.S. academic community who remember these "good old days" of well-behaved foreign students and who hold to standards or ideals formed back then. Their standards fail to take account of the fact that today's foreign students include many who are young, not especially well prepared or motivated for academic work, and intensely concerned with certain political issues.

The second factor that helps explain the higher standards some people hold for foreign students is that it is simply more inconvenient to deal with foreign students' problems than it is to deal with U.S. students' problems. There are established procedures, trained people, and commonly accepted approaches for coping with U.S. students' personal problems, political activities, financial difficulties, and so on. Foreign students' problems, although they may be identical to U.S. students' problems, are more difficult and time-consuming to cope with or solve. In part, this is simply because the students are foreign. This means that their basic ideas and perceptions may be harder to understand. They may not be able to express themselves well in American English; their ways of explaining themselves may be unfamiliar; and it may be harder to "read between the lines" of what they say. Furthermore, there is usually an absence or a shortage of established procedures, trained people and/or commonly accepted approaches for dealing with foreign students' problems.

Third, there is, naturally, less widespread understanding of the reasons underlying the behavior of students from abroad. U.S. academic personnel live in the U.S. and understand, more or less, the social forces influencing young people who grow up here. They can tolerate behavior that they would rather not encounter, because they can more or less understand how it comes to happen, and they can explain it to themselves without attributing it to the personal defects of individual students. In the case of foreign students, though, little if anything may be known about cultural or social factors that would help account for the existence of any particular problem or undesirable attitude or behavior. All that is evident is that the student's presence is somehow inconvenient, and the individual student is the one on whom responsibility for the inconvenience is most readily placed.

Fourth, there is simple prejudice. The attitudes and behaviors of U.S. students, inconvenient though they may sometimes be, are considered somehow "natural" or "right." Foreign students' attitudes and behavior are viewed less charitably. Foreign students are seen by some people here as underdeveloped people from underdeveloped countries, people who do not know how to act "right" and need to learn how to act if they are going to live in the U.S.

Of course, double standards occur naturally in human thinking. We can understand that. When these double standards lead to unfair judgments and behaviors, though, people concerned with justice will examine their standards and try to make them more fair. People who work in the field of educational exchange have a particular interest in ridding their own thinking of double standards that are unfair to foreign students, and in gently helping their colleagues in the academic community to do the same.

Organizations in International Educational Exchange

African-American Institute (AAI), 833 United Nations Plaza, New York, N.Y. 10017

America-Mideast Educational and Training Services, Inc. (AMID-EAST), 1717 Massachusetts Avenue Suite 100, Washington, D.C. 20036

American Association of Collegiate Registrars and Admissions Officers (AACRAO), One Dupont Circle, N.W., Suite 330, Washington, D.C. 20036

American Council for Nationalities Service, 20 W. 40th Street, New York, N.Y. 10018

Institute of International Education (IIE), 809 United Nations Plaza, New York, N.Y. 10017

Latin American Scholarship Program of American Universities (LAS-PAU), 25 Mt. Auburn Street, Cambridge, Massachusetts 02138

National Association for Foreign Student Affairs (NAFSA), 1860 19th Street N.W., Washington, D.C. 20009

Test of English as a Foreign Language (TOEFL), Box 899, Princeton, N.J. 08540

NAFSA Principles for International Educational Exchange

PRINCIPLES FOR INSTITUTIONS

The movement of students and scholars across community, cultural, geographic, and national boundaries has been recognized for centuries as essential to the discovery of truth, new knowledge, and the means of applying what is learned abroad to human enrichment and progress. In the second half of this century the interchange of students and scholars has grown steadily, become more formalized and an increasing influence upon U.S. education and the society as a whole. Indeed, the significance of the interdependence between nations, peoples, and world systems has brought international education into the very mainstream of higher education planning and requirements.

Programs of international educational exchange take many forms and are located in institutions of divergent purposes, sizes, and settings. Regardless of form and content the value of any program can be realized only when a college or university has made a conscious decision to be involved in international educational exchange and has made a commitment of resources commensurate with the nature and scope of that exchange. Such recognition and commitment require adherence to the following institution-wide principles:

1. The institution should have a clearly stated policy, endorsed by the governing board, setting forth the goals and objectives of the international educational program or programs developed by the

---

Reprinted by permission of the National Association for Foreign Student Affairs, 1860 19th Street N.W., Washington, D.C. 20009

institution. This policy should be manifest in the institution's planning and budgeting. Personnel and program resources—administrative and academic— should be sufficient to assure that the program can be operated in ways consistent with the principles presented in this document.

2. The executive staff of the institution should discuss with the faculty and administrative staff the implications of the international educational exchange policy for the academic programs and academic staff.

3. Programs in international educational exchange should be closely related to and consistent with the basic purposes and strengths of the institution.

4. Regardless of program size, the institution should acknowledge its responsibility to demonstrate sensitivity to cultural needs— social, religious, dietary, and housing. These factors must be accounted for in the planning and execution of the program.

5. Special services required by involvement in international educational exchange should be performed by personnel who are trained for their particular responsibilities, and institutional policy should ensure that faculty and administrative staff receive appropriate training for the activities they manage.

6. Administrative staff and faculty should seek to develop and maintain respect and sensitivity toward those from different cultures in the execution of their responsibilities for international educational exchange programs.

7. The institution should periodically evaluate programs, policies, and services in light of established goals, and regularly review those goals.

PRINCIPLES FOR THE
ADMISSION OF FOREIGN STUDENTS

Foreign citizens have usually been educated in school systems that vary from those in the United States. As a result, students from other countries are often unfamiliar with U.S. procedures and terminology. Institutions that admit foreign students must develop a sensitive and flexible admissions policy that reflects an awareness of different academic backgrounds and personal expectations.

To assist institutions in establishing a sound admissions policy and an effective admissions system, criteria for ethical recruitment were developed at a Wingspread colloquium in March 1980. These criteria, known as the "Wingspread Principles," are presented in *Foreign Student Recruitment: Realities and Recommendations,* and are incorporated in the following principles:

1. The admissions goals and policies for foreign students should be related directly to overall institutional goals and policies and include:

   a. The academic characteristics of students to whom admission is offered.

   b. The level—graduate or undergraduate—of students sought.

   c. Geographical areas to be emphasized or discouraged.

   d. The number of students desired (as a proportion of the student body).

   e. The extent to which the institution will make financial resources available to foreign students.

2. Admissions materials should be thorough, complete, and clearly written; they should be sensitive to candidates' unfamiliarity with U.S. education and lack of facility in the English language. Care should be taken to include:

   a. Detailed information about the admissions requirements and procedures.

   b. Candid, pertinent, and current information so that students unfamiliar with United States higher education may make informed academic judgments.

   c. Realistic information about full costs of study and living expenses, as well as the availability of financial aid.

   d. English language requirements and, if admitted initially for an English language training program, the degree of commitment the institution accepts for subsequent education of the student in another of its academic programs.

   e. Specific information about requirements of academic programs.

   f. Complete information regarding the conditions of admissions and acceptance, deposits, orientation, and all steps to be followed prior to arrival.

3. Recruitment of foreign students for both academic and English language training programs must be conducted in an ethical, responsible manner.

a. The student's educational goals must be ascertained and a responsible judgment made about whether they can be achieved at the accepting institution.

b. Admissions decisions should be made using complete files including academic documents, English proficiency reports, and other supporting materials.

c. Admissions responsibilities, including issuance of the visa eligibility certificate, should never be delegated to third parties outside the institution.

d. Applicants to an English language training program must be given full information about the extent of the institution's commitment to admit such applicants subsequently to another of its academic programs or provide assistance in obtaining admission to another institution.

4. The foreign admissions process should be conducted by personnel who are trained and competent in the interpretation of foreign educational records. These duties may be conducted on a full- or part-time basis as required by the size of the effort.

a. At the undergraduate level, foreign student admissions—usually a highly centralized process—should be enhanced by faculty advice.

b. In foreign graduate admissions, where deans' offices and faculty committees often play an important role, the advice and recommendations of admissions staff should be carefully considered in the decision process. The important contribution each individual can bring to the admissions decisions should be recognized.

c. Special reference resources should be acquired and new materials acquired as they become available.

d. Admissions personnel should call on the expertise of individuals on the campus, elsewhere, or abroad who can assist in providing sound evaluations.

5. The functions of the admissions office should be coordinated with those units responsible for English language training, academic programs, and student advising services, and there should be regular contact and sharing of information among those responsible for these functions.

6. The institution's foreign student program should be studied periodically in order to formulate any needed adjustments to

admissions criteria, procedures and processes:

a. Entering characteristics should be correlated periodically with student retention and other measures of performance.

b. Students should be queried periodically about reactions to admissions materials and procedures.

c. Other campus offices as well as cooperating agencies should be queried about the effectiveness of the admissions materials and procedures.

PRINCIPLES FOR ENGLISH PROGRAMS AND DETERMINATION OF ENGLISH PROFICIENCY

An extremely important factor in determining whether the presence of foreign students at a college or university will be a mutually beneficial experience for the students and the institution is the students' ability to use the English language. A student who cannot communicate adequately with faculty, staff, or fellow students will encounter significant difficulties in carrying out even limited daily activities. Moreover, serious deficiencies in English will hamper a student in pursuing an academic program at any level. For those students serving as graduate teaching assistants, the ability to speak English effectively in a classroom is especially critical.

For these reasons, an institution must carefully evaluate the English proficiency (overall ability to use the language) of prospective students when they are being considered for admission. In evaluating English proficiency, both level and field of study should be considered, since the most critical question to be answered is how well the student will be able to cope with a specific program at a given institution. Students whose English proficiency seems adequate for a regular academic program often need an English support course or courses in order to function more efficiently in the classroom or to meet an institutional English requirement. Institutions that maintain a policy of admitting foreign students who are qualified academically but who have limited or minimal skills in English must provide half-time or full-time (intensive) programs in English as a second language or refer students to English training programs where they can receive adequate instruction.

In an effort to establish guidelines by which institutions can evaluate their own or other English programs, NAFSA supports the following principles. These standards apply first to the question of determining English language proficiency and then to the training programs themselves. Except where specifically noted, these principles are meant to apply both to academic institutions and to private, proprietary organizations which offer English training programs.

Determining English proficiency

1. The procedures and criteria established for determining English proficiency should be clearly defined. While these procedures should be uniform and comprehensive, they must take into consideration differences presented by at least three common situations:

a. For students being admitted directly from overseas, English proficiency should be determined on the basis of results from widely accepted tests designed for this purpose.

b. For students who have enrolled in intensive English language programs conducted by the institution to which they are applying, additional information should be sought regarding the students' overall use of English, specific strengths and weaknesses, and motivation for continued improvement. In this regard there should be close communication between the admissions office and the English language program.

c. For students who have been enrolled in intensive English language programs at other institutions or at private language schools, similar information indicating level of English language proficiency should be sought. Admissions personnel should seek the assistance of any specialists in English as a second language at their institutions for guidance in interpreting such information.

2. Institutions should periodically assess their capacity to successfully determine English proficiency of prospective foreign students in light of the students' performance in subsequent academic programs.

English support courses

Students with sufficient command of English to begin regular academic work at a college or university frequently require additional training to prepare them for tasks encountered during their program of studies. This training is best provided through English support courses taken in conjunction with regular academic courses in the students' fields. These English courses should address the special needs of students whose native language is not English. They typically range from courses which are the equivalent of freshman English to advanced courses in technical English for graduate students.

3. After admission, the institution should employ effective procedures to identify those students who require some specialized training in English in light of the specific course of studies to be pursued. Special care should be taken to provide training in oral English skills for foreign graduate students assigned as teaching assistants.

4. Support courses should be designed and taught by individuals with training in the teaching of English as a second language.

Intensive English programs

The purpose of an intensive English language program is to develop and strengthen the English skills of persons whose native language is not English, usually in preparation for pursuing an academic program at the graduate or undergraduate level. Such individuals generally do not have sufficient command of English to begin regular academic work at a college or university. Some programs administered by colleges and universities enroll only students who have received academic admission to the institution but require short-term training, often in the summer. Most programs at academic institutions maintain year-round schedules and enroll people at varying levels of proficiency who intend to enter degree programs at the same or other institutions. Finally, a large number of programs are administered by private organizations. These latter programs, often housed at academic institutions, enroll students who must all continue their academic studies elsewhere. Based on experience from many established programs, it is not unrealistic to expect students who begin at the lowest levels to require a full calendar year to reach levels of proficiency sufficient to begin academic work.

5. Intensive English programs should establish clear goals and objectives for the training they provide. In the most general terms, these goals would be to provide sufficient and appropriate training to enable students to meet test score requirements established by the institutions they plan to attend.

6. In order to achieve these goals, intensive English programs should receive adequate support from their sponsoring institutions. Although no single administrative pattern is required, intensive programs should be sufficiently independent to permit the smooth functioning of all activities and units.

7. The director and core faculty of an intensive English program should have principal commitments to the program. The director should have advanced academic training in the teaching of English as a second language and have teaching and administrative experience, if possible, including overseas experience. Part-time instructors, especially if they are graduate students in a university program, should be taking or have taken graduate work in the teaching of English as a second language.

8. To ensure that students will be adequately prepared for an academic program, the syllabus of an intensive English program should include training in a variety of skills. The most basic are listening (understanding spoken English) and reading (understanding written English). Also of importance for academic work are speaking (in both formal and informal settings) and writing (primarily expository writing needed in most fields of study).

PRINCIPLES FOR FOREIGN STUDENT/SCHOLAR SERVICES

An institution that enrolls foreign students or invites foreign scholars should recognize that individuals from different cultures and educational systems have special needs for advice and assistance. These needs must be met by services that are organized, directed, and funded by the host institution. The scope and level of such services is to some extent dependent on the number of foreign students and scholars. Regardless of their number, however, the presence of foreign students and scholars requires certain basic levels of support which enable them to function successfully in U.S. colleges or universities. The following principles concern the provision of these essential services:

1. The host institution should state clearly its intentions to provide special services for the foreign students and scholars it brings to its campus. These services should include:

   a. Advisory and counseling services.

   b. Mandated and technical services in compliance with U.S. regulations.

c. Coordination and liaison with the community.

2. Regardless of the number of foreign students and scholars, the level of funding, or other circumstances, there must be one unit in the host institution that is responsible for coordinating these services, and there should be clear and widely acknowledged designation of responsibility for these services.

  a. These duties may require full- or part-time staff, depending upon the size of the clientele. Where possible, it is highly desirable to have a single individual or office designated to provide these advisory services.

  b. The staff should be knowledgeable about U.S. immigration law and regulations.

3. The institution should provide ample professional services which are fully accessible to foreign students and scholars. The intention of these services is to assure that maximum benefit is derived from the educational experience. The advisory services must seek to remove impediments and to solve problems on behalf of these individuals.

  a. The advisory staff must work closely with other campus and community resources which can be of assistance before arrival and throughout the individual's stay.

  b. An orientation program that introduces students to the physical environment, registration procedures, academic policies, housing, counseling and health services, visa requirements and INS regulations, financial services, and social and intercultural activities should be provided.

  c. Advisory services should be provided on an ongoing basis with respect to personal counseling, emergency needs, institutional policies, preparation for departure, and re-entry to home countries upon completion of stay.

  d. The advisory staff serve both the institution and the students and scholars it enrolls; they should, therefore, perform an intermediary role and be a channel of communication between those individuals and outside agencies or institutions.

  e. The advisory staff should seek to bring an intercultural dimension to the educational programs of the institution and the general life of the community.

   f. Advisory services should include academic advising— performed either by faculty members or foreign student advisers.

4. The advisory staff should exercise their duties in an ethical and professional manner. They must:

   a. Adhere to the regulations of the U.S. government, especially those of the Immigration and Naturalization Service.

   b. Decline awards and unethical requests for service.

PRINCIPLES FOR THE PROVISION OF COMMUNITY SERVICES AND PROGRAMS

The presence of foreign students and scholars on campus and in the community involves cross-cultural relationships and provides opportunities for increased global awareness. Individual contacts and the sharing of a variety of social and professional activities provide the opportunity for mutual appreciation of different cultural and national aspirations.

Although it may serve a wider constituency at the state or national level, the college or university is an integral part of the community in which it exists. Colleges and universities which enroll foreign students and scholars should make, in cooperation with the community, every effort to assist these students in their adjustment to life in an American community. They may also enhance the education of foreign students and scholars by offering a variety of experiences, both on campus and in the community, which will ensure that optimum benefit is derived from the period of study in the United States.

Institutions should be receptive to approaches from the community and should, if necessary, take the initiative in establishing a relationship with the community (a) to explain the needs of foreign students and scholars, (b) to identify the resources represented by foreign students, and (c) to explore and make full use of the willingness and ability of the community to provide services and programs.

Through the office of the foreign student adviser or its equivalent, institutions should provide assistance, advice, and information as requested by the community for the development of programs and services for foreign students and scholars. These efforts should be evaluated periodically.

Community programs and services should adhere to the following principles:

1. Community groups and organizations should seek to provide programs and services that enhance the experience of the foreign students and scholars while increasing the level of international and intercultural awareness in the community.

2. Community programs and services should be developed in cooperation with the university office that provides on-campus service to foreign students and scholars. Each should be competently designed and conducted and, where possible, coordinated with other community efforts.

3. Community programs must embrace a sensitivity to, and appreciation of, the religious, cultural, and national backgrounds of foreign participants and a proper regard for confidential personal information that may be offered by foreign and American participants.

4. Community groups and organizations should provide professional training for volunteers and paid staff to ensure that programs are competently administered and community resources effectively used.

5. Community groups and organizations should periodically evaluate their programs, policies, and services in light of their established goals and the changing needs of foreign students and scholars.

PRINCIPLES FOR U.S. STUDY ABROAD

One of the most effective ways to increase U.S. understanding of other languages and cultures and to improve our ability to function effectively in this interdependent world is to provide individuals with opportunities to study abroad. By living and studying in another country people learn to live with and appreciate different points of view and gain a more global perspective on life's challenges and opportunities.

The insititution that endorses the concept of study abroad should provide some form of basic advisory services. Many opportunities exist for American students interested in studying abroad—sponsored programs of their own institution, programs sponsored cooperatively with other institutions, and hundreds of direct opportunities which may or may not have U.S. institutional sponsorship.

These principles apply to the delivery of advisory services as well as to the direct administration of a study abroad program or co-sponsorship of a program with other institutions.

1. Within the context of its overall international educational objectives, an institution should have a clearly stated policy about its intentions and goals for facilitating study abroad.

Advisory services for study abroad

2. Recognizing that programs and advising may be handled by various people on campus, there should be a central point of access to useful information about overseas opportunities. A library of essential study abroad information materials should be maintained.

3. Faculty and staff members who are responsible for advising should be identified and listed in campus reference literature. These individuals should be given opportunities to develop their abilities to provide sound, knowledgeable, and objective advice about study abroad programs. Important components of advising include the following:

   a. Clarifying objectives for wanting to go abroad.
   b. Identifying opportunities that are educationally sound and culturally beneficial.
   c. Determining the quality, value, and appropriateness of a particular study abroad experience.
   d. Coordinating evaluation of students' educational background with admissions personnel of foreign institutions.
   e. Understanding the implications of a particular study abroad experience on graduation requirements, transfer credit, and financial aid.

4. Returning students should be asked to provide evaluations to enable study abroad advisers to determine the usefulness of the program for those students and possible future participants in that program, and to evaluate the usefulness of the advisory service they received before going abroad.

Co-sponsoring study abroad programs administered by other institutions

In order to encourage study abroad or broaden the options readily available to its students, a number of institutions have elected to join consortia or co-sponsor study abroad programs in which the institution handles program administration. A consortium or co-sponsorship arrangement for study abroad should provide opportunities that are consistent with the institution's overall academic objectives, requirements, and standards; the program should be administered in accordance with the principles for study abroad program administration (see below); and the home campus role in the co-sponsorship should be evaluated periodically by faculty, staff, and students to determine if the objectives are being met.

Administration of study abroad programs

Institutions administer study abroad programs in order to establish direct control over the development and provision of a specific kind of overseas learning experience. Many different kinds of institutions operate programs, including U.S. colleges and universities, foreign universities and companies, and proprietary organizations. The types of programs and amounts of structure and support services vary tremendously. Despite the wide range, all should be administered according to the following principles.

5. The purposes and specific educational objectives of the program should be carefully developed and clearly stated in the program bulletin and promotional materials.

6. Accurate, honest, and complete information should be provided to prospective applicants describing the nature and scope of the program including its opportunities and limitations, how and where instruction will be given, the relationship, if any, to a foreign institution, grading practices, significant differences between a home campus experience and what can be expected abroad, information about local attitudes and mores, local living conditions, and the extent of responsibility assumed by the program for housing participants.

7. Applicants should be screened to ensure that participants have the maturity, adequate language proficiency, academic background and achievement, and motivation necessary for success in the type of program and place of study.

8. The program should include an orientation, both predeparture and ongoing, which assists participants in making appropriate personal, social, and academic adjustments. Programs maintaining centers abroad should provide counseling and supervisory services

at the foreign center, with special attention to the problems peculiar to the location and nature of the program.

9. The program should encourage extensive and effective use of the unique physical, human, and cultural resources of the host environment, and the academic rigor of the program should be comparable to that at the home campus. There should be clearly defined criteria and policies for judging performance and assigning credit in accordance with prevailing standards and practices at the home institution.

10. Administrative arrangements (such as housing, transportation, and finances) and support services (such as counseling and health services) made both in the U.S. and at the program location abroad should be managed effectively by carefully selected and qualified staff who have both appropriate academic and administrative experience necessary to perform the work.

11. Programs should be evaluated periodically by student participants, program administrators, and a faculty advisory committee to determine the extent to which objectives and purposes are being met. Changes should be made in light of the findings.

List of Institutional Personnel
FSA's Might Want to Know

Chief executive officer

Chief academic officer

Chief student affairs officer

Chief business officer

All people in own chain of command, up to the chief executive

People responsible for each of the following:

    admissions

    foreign admissions

    registration

    student record keeping

    student accounts

    financial aid

    housing

    student activities

    student health

    campus security

    public information

    alumni affairs

    fund-raising

    institutional relations with the state and federal governments

Heads (deans, chairpeople) of all academic units where foreign students are enrolled

As many faculty as possible

Academic advisers (if different from faculty)

Outline for a Session on Students from Country X

The session's leader can explain the purpose of the session and provide some general background:

1. location of the country (having a map posted is very helpful)

2. number of students from Country X at the institution—the total plus breakdowns by sex, level of study, field of study, marital status, sources of financial support, and type of housing (on- or off-campus)

Members of a panel of students from Country X can then give brief comments on the following points:

1. educational background of students from Country X

    a. characteristics of Country X's educational system

        i. selectivity

        ii. teaching methods

        iii. mental skills rewarded

        iv. daily life of a secondary or university student

    b. reasons for coming to the United States and to the particular U.S. institution

    c. educational and occupational aspirations

2. the experience of Country X students at the particular institution

    a. initial experiences and reactions

        i. to the United States in general

        ii. to the particular institution

b. comparison of the institution's academic system with the one at home

 i. academic advising

 ii. selecting courses

 iii. class attendance

 iv. behavior of teachers

 v. behavior of students in class toward the teacher and toward other students

 vi. examinations

 vii. assignments

 viii. use of library

 iv. grades

c. comparison of local "student life" with that at home

 i. student service offices

 ii. general administrative procedures (registration, paying bills, getting a residence hall room, etc.)

 iii. social life

3. things about the local situation that commonly seem unpleasant to students from Country X

4. things students from Country X need to learn in order to accommodate themselves to the local situation

5. things North Americans are advised to keep in mind when interacting with students from Country X

6. questions and answers

A session following this outline will usually take at least 90 minutes. It is best if the panelists have seen the topics beforehand and prepared their remarks. Without fairly directive leadership from the chair, the session might go well beyond 90 minutes.

The Communicative Style of Americans

According to the communications scholar Dean Barnlund, "communicative style" refers to

1. the topics people prefer to discuss,
2. people's favorite forms of verbal interaction (ritual, repartee, argument, self-disclosure),
3. the depth of involvement people seek from each other,
4. communication channels people tend to rely on (vocal, verbal, physical), and
5. the level of meaning to which people are generally attuned (the factual or the emotional content of messages).

When people with differing communicative styles interact, they frequently feel ill-at-ease, and they often misjudge or misunderstand each other. To help understand why that happens and to try to reduce the communications problems that arise when it does happen, it is helpful if foreigners (anywhere, not just in the U.S.) know something about the communicative style of the local people and the way it compares with their own communicative style. With that knowledge, the foreigners will be better able to understand what is happening when they are dealing with the local people and will know some of the ways in which the local people are likely to misunderstand or misjudge them.

Here are some *generalizations* (subject to exceptions) about the communicative style of Americans:

Note: This is adapted from the *Handbook for Foreign Students and Professionals*, published by the Office of International Education and Services at the University of Iowa.

1. *Preferred topics.* In casual conversation (what they call "small talk"), Americans prefer to talk about the weather, sports, jobs, mutual acquaintances, and past experiences, especially ones they have in common with their conversation partners. As they grow up, most Americans are warned *not* to discuss politics or religion, at least not with people they do not know rather well, because politics and religion are considered controversial topics. Sex, bodily functions, and perceived personal inadequacies are considered very personal topics and are likely to be discussed only between people who know each other very well. (Younger people generally discuss sex more freely than older people do.)

By contrast, people in some other cultures are taught to believe that politics and/or religion are good conversation topics, and they may have different ideas about what topics are too "personal" to discuss with others.

2. *Favorite form of verbal interaction.* In the typical conversation between Americans, no one talks for very long at a time. Participants in conversation "take turns" frequently, usually after the speaker has spoken only a few sentences. Americans prefer to avoid arguments; if argument is unavoidable, they prefer it to be restrained, carried on in a normal conversational tone and volume. Americans are generally rather impatient with "ritual" conversational exchanges. (Only a very few of them are common: "How are you?" "Fine, thank you, how are you?" "Fine." "It was very nice to meet you." "I hope to see you again.")

People from other countries may be more accustomed to speaking and listening for longer periods when they are in a conversation; they may be accustomed to more ritual interchanges (about the health of family members, for example) than Americans are. They may enjoy argument, even vigorous argument, of a kind that Americans are likely to find unsettling.

3. *Depth of involvement preferred.* Americans do not generally expect very much personal involvement from conversational partners. "Small talk"—without long silences, which provoke uneasiness—is enough to keep matters going smoothly. It is only with very close friends (or with complete strangers whom they do not expect to see again) that Americans generally expect to discuss personal topics.

Some people from other countries prefer even less personal involvement than Americans do and rely more on ritual interchanges. Others come from countries where much more personal involvement is sought, as one wants to learn as much as possible about another person in order to open the possibility of developing a close relationship.

4. *Channels preferred*. The ideal among Americans is to be somewhat verbally adept, speaking in moderate tones, using relatively few and restrained gestures of the arms and hands. They do not touch each other very often.

By contrast, others might prefer even quieter conversation, less talking, and even more restrained gestures. Or they might be accustomed to louder voices, many people talking at once, vigorous use of hands and arms to convey meanings or add emphasis, and/or more touching between conversation partners.

5. *Level of meaning emphasized*. Americans are generally taught to believe in the "scientific method" of understanding the world around them, so they tend to look for specific facts and physical or quantifiable evidence to support viewpoints. (Underlying this search for facts is the assumption that there are "truths" about people and nature that can be discovered by means of "objective" inquiry that is carried out by trained people using "scientific" means of measurement or observation.)

Compared to Americans, people from some other countries might pay more attention to the emotional content or the human feelings aspects of a message and be less concerned with what Americans would call "facts." (They may not assume the existence of an objective "truth," but may suppose that "facts" are relative, depending on who is observing them.)

Many misjudgments and misunderstandings can arise from interactions between people who have different communicative styles. Here are some examples:

—Foreign visitors in the U.S. might hear little but "small talk" among Americans and erroneously conclude that Americans are not intellectually capable of anything more than simple talk about such subjects as the weather, sports, teachers or their own social activities. The conclusion that Americans are intellectually inferior is also reached by many people who regard argument as a favorite form of interaction and who find that Americans are often not very adept at arguing.

—Responding to people who customarily speak little and who rely heavily on ritual conversation, Americans might use the labels "shy," "too formal," or "too polite."

—Vigorous arguing (with raised voices and much use of hands and arms, and perhaps more than one person talking at a time) of the kind that is "natural" to some people may alarm Americans, who expect violence, or at least long-lasting anger, to follow from loud disagreements.

—What Americans might regard favorably as "keeping cool"—that is, not being drawn into an argument, not raising the voice, looking always for the "facts"—might be seen by others as coldness and a sort of lack of humanness. Conversely, Americans are likely to see those who do not "keep cool" as being "too emotional."

—Embarrassment or unease almost always result when someone raises a discussion topic that the other person thinks is inappropriate for the particular setting or relationship.

—Americans are likely to view a very articulate person with some suspicion.

These are but a few of the many misjudgments that arise between Americans and people in the U.S. from other countries. It can be very helpful to be aware of the differences in communicative style that produce them. *Talking about differences in communicative style,* when such a difference seems to be causing problems, is usually a good way to reduce the negative effects of the differences.

K

The INS and the FSA

An organization is a group of people operating under many kinds of influences. These influences include job descriptions, supervisory practices, in-service training techniques, statements of policy and procedure, organizational structure, and so on. Many of the influences on the behavior of people within organizations stem from conscious decisions made by people who are responsible for assuring that each person working for the organization performs his or her duties in a particular way.

Other influences on the behavior of people within organizations are unplanned. They do not stem from conscious decisions made by supervisory personnel or other authorities. Examples are the personalities of the individual employees and social or political events occurring outside the organization but affecting its operations.

When dealing with an organization, it is very helpful to understand those factors which influence the behavior of the people who work for it. After all, one is dealing not with an organization, but with *individual people* who are employed there. It helps to have an idea what influences those people to act in the way they do.

Many people in the field of educational exchange in the U.S. have frequent occasion to work with the Immigration and Naturalization Service. The purpose of this brief essay is to help those who have contact with the INS to understand the position and viewpoint of INS personnel. Such an understanding can aid in establishing and maintaining relations with the INS which, if not always harmonious and cooperative, will be as fruitful as possible.

Note: This article originally appeared in the *NAFSA Newsletter* for January, 1976.

This essay begins with information about the hierarchy and some characteristics of the INS. That is followed by some very specific suggestions that are intended to help put one's understanding of the INS to constructive use.

THE INS

Hierarchy and responsibilities

Like most large federal agencies in the U.S., the INS is organized into national, regional, and district levels. Foreign student advisers deal most frequently with the *district* office having jurisdiction over the place where their school is located. It is helpful, however, to have a knowledge of regional and national INS operations.

If an adviser has dealings with INS national headquarters, it will probably be to obtain information about immigration law and procedure or to question an action taken by his or her district office. INS headquarters in Washington employs lawyers who are very well-versed in immigration law, and it is among their responsibilities to answer questions that the public, including foreign student advisers, might have about immigration law and procedure. Such questions should be addressed to the General Counsel, Immigration and Naturalization Service, 425 Eye St., N.W., Washington, D.C. 20536.

The lawyers on the INS staff, like all other INS employees, have very heavy workloads—a topic discussed in more detail below. Since they are so busy, inquiries addressed to them may not receive replies for a considerable period of time. Questions about district decisions are usually addressed to the Assistant Commissioner for Adjudication at the above address. As is discussed below, instances do arise where district office decisions do not have the agreement of headquarters, and in such cases the headquarters office is sometimes empowered to overrule the district office. It can at least request a reconsideration of the district office's decision.

When the national office is asked to review a decision taken at the district level, the district office is notified of the request. District office personnel might not welcome the fact that the questioner has "gone over their heads" to seek reversal or reconsideration of their decision. That fact should be kept in mind when one is considering a request to the central office that might reflect unfavorably on the district office. At the least, the district office should be informed when a question to headquarters is being contemplated and should be given the opportunity to reconsider its decision before headquarters is asked to become involved.

Dealings with *regional* INS offices may resemble those with the national office—i.e., they may involve efforts to clarify law and procedure, or to seek reversal of a district office decision. The latter may involve a formal appeal. Certain decisions taken at the district level may be appealed to the regional commissioner. The alien affected by such a district office decision will be notified by the district office when an appeal to the regional commissioner is appropriate and will be given instructions for appealing.

It is with the district INS office that the adviser deals on a regular basis. Thus it helps to know what functions are carried out in a district office and who is responsible for carrying them out.

The district office is headed by the District Director, or "DD." The Deputy Director is second in command. The two main areas of work that go on in a district office and that involve the clients of a foreign student adviser are *examinations*, carried out by people called "examiners," and *investigations*, carried out by people who are called "investigators."

Immigration examiners, who are sometimes called "adjudicating officers," are in a division of the INS that is called "Travel Control." Travel Control, or "TC," is concerned with maintaining records on aliens who are in the U.S. and with "adjudicating" aliens' applications for benefits under the immigration law. Immigration examiners, then, are responsible for processing routine applications from nonimmigrants—applications for extension of stay, permission to work, adjustment of status, and so on. Some of the routine applications may be sent elsewhere to be processed. They may go to a border post along the U.S.-Canadian frontier, to an international airport where INS employees process them when they are not occupied with incoming traffic, or to a "regional adjudication center," where INS officers work on applications coming from a number of different district offices. When routine applications are "remoted" from a district office they are often sent in "batches" that have been allowed to accumulate for a period of time. Delays can result from this process.

Decisions emanating from district offices generally appear over the name of the District Director, even though he himself may not have been involved in the making of each decision.

Immigration investigators are responsible for looking into cases where violations of law appear to have taken place. Such violations include accepting unauthorized employment, failure to obtain an extension of permission for temporary stay, and so on.

Only a small portion of the work of immigration examiners and investigators concerns foreign students and exchange visitors. The bulk of their work relates to aliens in other categories.

In addition to the DD, his deputy, the examiners, and the investigators (whose number in each district vary according to the volume of work the particular office receives), a district office is staffed by clerical personnel and a "contact agent." The contact agent works at the front desk, meeting the public to answer questions and assist in carrying out the person-to-person business that takes place in the office.

As is the case in any hierarchical organization, more discretionary authority lies with those higher up in a district office than with those lower down. While a clerical person or a contact agent might be able to answer questions of *fact* (e.g., what form should be used by an H-1 alien to extend his permission to stay), he or she will be unable to respond to inquiries concerning the disposition of a particular case (e.g., will you restore Juan Doe to F-1 status if he submits an I-20 and a letter explaining the lapse in his status) or any matter that involves an exercise in discretion. Examiners exercise more decision-making power than contact agents, deputy directors more than examiners, and DD's more than their deputies.

In dealing with a district office the adviser should know the position in the hierarchy of the INS person he needs to talk to concerning various kinds of questions. It is a waste of the adviser's time to ask a contact agent to exercise discretion in a particular case, and it is a waste of the DD's time to entertain a request for a new supply of I-20 forms.

FACTORS INFLUENCING INS BEHAVIOR

The charge of the organization

The INS is a law enforcement agency. It is responsible for controlling the entry of aliens into the U.S., monitoring them while they are here, and assuring that they depart when they are supposed to (unless they entered as immigrants or have adjusted status). In doing this work the INS follows written guidelines, including the Immigration and Naturalization Act, the Code of Federal Regulations, and Operations Instructions disseminated from Washington to regional and district offices. In a given case, INS personnel are responsible for considering a set of facts in relation to a set of written guidelines, and making a decision that is in accordance with those guidelines.

Like other contemporary U.S. law enforcement agencies, the INS accounts for its performance primarily in terms of quantities. How many aliens were inspected at ports of entry? How many applications for benefits under the INA were processed? How many illegal entrants were located? How many people were deported? The INS's annual report gives a good portrayal of the indices it uses to measure its performance. In sum, they indicate that the INS is concerned with the efficient application of immigration law.

Manpower problems

The INS considers itself overworked, understaffed and underfunded. According to a recent Commissioner of Immigration some aspects of the INS's workload have grown by a factor of ten over the past decade while its manpower and operating budget have hardly grown at all. Given that and given the priorities the INS has set for itself, the INS personnel that the foreign student adviser deals with have too much work to do. To cope with it, INS personnel learn to live with long delays, lost papers, and decisions made with inadequate time for the thorough consideration that might be warranted. INS personnel (like many foreign student advisers) often see themselves as doing the best they can do in the face of overwhelming odds.

In addition to the perceived shortage of personnel, the INS's manpower problems have another aspect. In the early 1970's efforts were made by the Administration to lower the average grade level of federal government employees. That meant that a job formerly carried out by a person with a certain amount of training and experience was turned over to a person with less training and experience. In many cases this meant that routine applications were being adjudicated by people with little or no experience in adjudicating applications. There was much on-the-job training at border posts, airports, and in the district offices. Through no fault of their own, INS personnel were thrust into positions for which they were less than adequately prepared. Errors and delays were not unusual results of this situation. The personnel concerned have tried hard to overcome this disadvantage, but their heavy workload has not made it easy.

External forces on the INS

No organization operates in a vacuum. Any organization, in order to continue to exist, must be responsive to influences that come upon it from without. The INS, like other organizations, is affected by the political, economic, and social tenor of the times.

One of the external factors affecting the INS is the economic situation of the U.S. and the world. When the economic situation is good, the INS is under less pressure to be stringent about allowing nonimmigrants to accept employment and about locating and removing illegal aliens. When the economic situation is unfavorable, pressure to prevent aliens from entering the labor market mounts.

Another external factor influencing the INS is the amount of isolationism perceived within the U.S. public. At some times non-Americans are more welcome here than at others. Some kinds of non-Americans may be more welcome than other kinds. The INS reacts to its perceptions of these sentiments.

Of course, there are other external factors which bear on the outlook and performance of the INS. Whatever the forces are, they come to bear on the INS in a variety of ways. They may come directly from the public, as when citizens express to the INS their concern about jobs that are being taken by aliens illegally in the country or about jobs that are not being done because aliens are being discouraged from entering the country to take them.

Popular concerns might also be brought to the attention of the INS through the Congress, whose members hear their constituents' opinions relating to aliens and convey them to the INS. Besides the Congress, other governmental agencies do work that involves the INS or the clientele of the INS. Examples are the Department of State, the Department of Labor, the Social Security Administration, and the Internal Revenue Service. All of these agencies may try to influence INS policies and behavior.

Thus, particular INS policies and decisions may be products of a complex interplay of influences that no one individual inside or outside the INS itself fully comprehends.

Headquarters-field relations

Like any large organization that has a central office in one place and "branch" offices elsewhere, the INS experiences what are called "headquarters-field problems." That is, policies, procedures or interpretations are disseminated from headquarters in the hope that they will be implemented in a uniform way in all the field offices (in this case, regional and district offices), so that the agency will have a uniform policy. What frequently happens, for a variety of reasons, is that implementation of the policy is *not* uniform. The field office may not understand the new policy in the way it was intended, or may pay less attention to it than the headquarters hoped it would, or may believe that specific local circumstances make it necessary to modify the new policy before it can be applied "realistically" in the area the field office serves.

Thus, in the case of the INS, it is not unusual to find that policies and interpretations *vary* among district offices and among regional offices, even though, in theory, all are implementing the same law according to the same criteria and procedures.

The influence of particular personalities

By means of its recruitment programs, training procedures, job descriptions, operating instructions, supervisory practices, and performance reviews, any organization seeks to assure *uniform* implementation of its policies. The purpose of an organization, after all, is to bring people together to work in cooperation—rather like the parts of a machine. The people are to fill *roles*, and the occupant of a role, like each part of the machine, is supposed to perform in certain consistent ways.

Of course, people are not machines. Therefore organizations, the INS among them, have to contend with particular personalities. Unlike machine parts, individual human beings have their own political viewpoints, temperaments, levels of tolerance, moods, and prejudices. Try though it might, an organization cannot completely remove the influence of particular personalities.

What all this means in the case of the INS is that variations occur not just between district offices, but *within* given offices. One immigration examiner might be more sympathetic toward foreign students than another. One DD may be difficult to deal with in interpersonal situations, while his succesor proves to be pleasant and cooperative.

U.S. immigration law leaves a large amount to the discretion of INS personnel. That fact, coupled with the fact of personality difference, can make for considerable variation in the treatment of foreign students and scholars among and within the various INS district offices.

Supervisors within the INS do not welcome these variations in the treatment of INS clients. They prefer uniformity. While District Directors, like most supervisors, generally believe that their staffs are doing the best they can under difficult circumstances, DD's appreciate hearing about decisions of their staffs when those decisions reflect great variation from other decisions made under similar sets of facts.

In this section we have reviewed some of the factors that influence the behavior of INS personnel. In the following section we will see how knowledge of these factors can be put to practical use in working with the INS.

BUILDING WORKING RELATIONS WITH THE INS

What kinds of relationships with the INS are possible? To suggest the *range* of possibilities that can be found, let us briefly consider two divergent types. Relations between various educational institutions and the INS can range from the pure *adversary model* to the pure *cooperation model*. These are theoretical models and are given here for purposes of discussion and illustration. They rarely exist in the real world, where relationships represent a combination of cooperative and adversary viewpoints and behavior.

According to the adversary model, the goals and methods of the INS and those of the educational institutions are generally antithetical to each other, so that continuing conflict, disagreement, and hard feelings between members of the two organizations is the normal state of affairs. In a situation where relations are of the adversary type, educational institutions tend to view the INS as an agency whose views are anti-foreign student and anti-education, whose general outlook is excessively limited, and whose procedures are time-consuming and unreasonable. Educational institutions cannot, in good conscience, cooperate with such an agency as this.

The INS, on the other hand, is thought to see educational institutions as gullible, soft-hearted agencies which are too naive to appreciate the economic and political forces that operate in the real world. Cooperation with such misguided institutions is, of course, very imprudent.

According to the cooperation model, the INS and educational institutions have a common interest in a well-enforced Immigration and Nationality Act, since that Act represents the "law of the land" where both the INS and the educational institutions exist and seek to pursue their respective ends. When differences of opinion do happen to arise, their strong concern for the maintenance of harmonious relations with the INS leads the educational institutions—which are not charged with law enforcement—to give unqualified acceptance to INS decisions.

Again, these are theoretical models. In the real world, relationships between educational institutions and the INS fall at different points on a continuum between the two extremes. Sometimes cooperation predominates and sometimes adversary behavior holds sway. While it is recognized by both parties that the INA is the law of the land, it is also recognized that reasonable people can differ as to the Act's proper application in a given case. Since the INS and the educational institutions do have differing goals and values, differences of opinion (whether serious or not) are likely to emerge at least from time to time. Even with these differences, people can work together cooperatively. This represents what might be called a moderate view. For readers who subscribe to the moderate view, the remainder of this essay provides guidelines and considerations for working as cooperatively as possible with the INS.

Know their organization and personnel

From what has been said already it is clear that prudent advisors will *know whom to deal with* when they have particular kinds of questions. This involves knowing the breakdown of responsibilities in the local district office. It also involves knowing which individuals in the district office (if one has a choice between individuals) have the discretion and the will to be the most helpful.

An adviser who does not know whom to talk to in his local office has a number of options:

—Telephone the INS and tell the person answering what the question concerns, then ask to whom it should be addressed. Be sure to ask the name of the person answering the question.

—Telephone an advisor at a large neighboring institution, assuming that he will have had extensive dealings with the local INS office and will be familiar with its personnel.

—Visit the INS office, explaining your role and your interest in understanding (1) how they operate and (2) how you, from their viewpoint, can do a good job.

—Call the District Director and invite him to send a representative of his office to your institution to meet you and some of your foreign students.

—Attend regional NAFSA conferences, to which local INS personnel are often invited.

In short, foreign student advisers are best able to have fruitful relations with the INS if they establish and continuously work to maintain a personal relationship with the appropriate local INS personnel. An adviser's skills in human relations are as helpful in dealing with the INS as they are in dealing with foreign students, community groups, and others.

Advisers' communications with the INS need not be restricted to asking questions and stating points of view on legal matters. They can also express appreciation for assistance or special help received from an INS representative. INS personnel, like everyone else, welcome such expressions.

Understand their viewpoint

In addition to knowing whom to deal with and attempting to deal with him in a constructive way, advisers had better remain aware of the way in which INS personnel perceive themselves, their work, FSA's, and an FSA's work. Remember that the INS is a law enforcement agency, not an educational institution or a social work organization. Remember that INS personnel see themselves as law enforcement agents. Be mindful that INS personnel are not responsible for the fact that the world is divided into sovereign countries or for the fact that the Immigration and Nationality Act is written as it is. Advisers' opinions on these matters should be directed to the Congress, not to INS personnel. Meanwhile, when dealing with the INS, advisers had best accept the spirit of the law. Finally, realize that INS personnel may have valid reasons for supposing that advisers are not as skeptical as they should be in championing the cause of a particular student or scholar.

Do your own work well

Advisers are more likely to be able to command the respect of local INS personnel if it is clear to the INS that they are approaching their responsibilities in a serious and professional manner. Such an approach would include these elements:

—Know as much as possible about immigration law and procedure, in order to know what points are at issue in a given case, to be able to ask informed questions, and to understand the answers. Advisers who are unfamiliar with the law can, of course, ask the INS to help them understand it. But they should not argue with the INS about points of law unless they know whereof they speak.

—Know what forms foreign students and scholars should use for what purposes and make sure those forms are properly and legibly executed before signing them and forwarding them to the INS.

—Maintain your integrity. An adviser's chances of working effectively with the INS are significantly reduced if the local INS office learns through experience that the adviser's judgments and recommendations are made without prudent consideration of a situation.

Know how to get outside help

Sometimes the adviser may know the INS has made an unfair decision, or may believe or suspect that it could have decided otherwise than it did, and would like INS to reconsider. What can be done?

An appeal or request for reconsideration is always possible. Appeals can be informal, usually in the form of a letter or a phone call to the appropriate INS employee. When formal appeals are in order, the INS so notifies the recipient of the unfavorable decision. Turning to outside influences and sources of information is also a possibility. As was mentioned earlier, the INS does not operate in a vacuum. Expressions of interests from Senators and Congressmen do get attention—of course they may get negative attention, and they may result in INS displeasure with the person who brought them about.

There are a large number of sources of information and assistance for working with the INS. Within NAFSA, they include foreign student advisers at other institutions and members of the Government Regulations Advisory Committee. Outside NAFSA, they include law school faculty, the counsel of educational institutions, political science faculty (especially those in constitutional law), legal aid societies, the American Civil Liberties Union, and, of course, lawyers.

Something should be said on the subject of lawyers, because it is a difficult matter of judgment to determine when a foreign student adviser or his client should seek professional legal assistance. Lawyers versed in immigration law are not available in many localities. Finding a lawyer who is both versed in immigration law and known to be effective in dealing with the INS is not always easy. Nonetheless, the effort to find one should be seriously considered when an adviser's client represents an extremely complicated case or a case whose outcome will affect only the client's private interests and not the interests of the educational institution.

Maintain your perspective

Some of the *dicta* we refer to in our daily lives are relevent for advisers who are working with the INS. They include these:

—You win some, you lose some.
—Life isn't fair.
—They're only doing their job.
—I have my bad days too.

Programming Considerations

Some questions to ask yourself in setting up a program might be:

1. **Identifying needs**—What do the people involved want and need?

   a. Who is the audience? Consider age, year in school, major, previous experience and knowledge of the area of the program, sex, cultural background, motivation, likes and dislikes.

   b. How big is the audience?

   c. What does the audience need? To be better students? To be better people? To be better citizens? To relate better to others? To be able to manage their lives better?

   d. What do the members of the audience want?

   e. What do we, the programmers, want to get out of the program? Learning about ourselves? Learning about others? Skills development in programming and leadership? A feeling of success? Recognition?

   f. What do other groups (staff, faculty, parents, etc.) want the audience to gain from their experience?

2. **Developing goals and objectives**—What do we want to do?

   a. Which of the needs identified are most important to the audience?

   b. Which areas of that need do we want to address?

   c. What do we want the audience to get out of the program?

3. **Organizing program plans**—What do we need to do to fulfill our objectives and goals?

a. *Scheduling.* When do we want to do the program? When will most people be able to come to the program? What else is going on then? Do we have time to make all the arrangements? Do we personally have enough time to do the program and fulfill our personal commitments?

b. *Facilities.* Where do we want to do the program? How big is the audience? What kind of setting do we want (informal, formal, indoors, outdoors, etc.)? What room or hall is available when we want to do the program?

c. *Budget.* How much money do we have to work with? How much will facilities, refreshments, publicity, speakers, equipment, etc., cost? How can we get more money if we need it? Do we want to charge admission? How much will the audience be willing to pay?

d. *Methods and resources.* What method will best help us achieve our objectives (lecture, film, party, discussion group, etc.)? What method will best be accepted by the audience? Where can we find needed resources (bands, speakers, equipment, films, etc.)? Are there contracts to be signed, arrangements to be made for resource people?

e. *Publicity.* What information do people need to know about the program? How can we best get that information to our audience? What can we do to attract people's attention? Do we need help in developing our publicity and where can we get it (artists, writers, printers, etc.)?

f. *Clean-up and follow-up.* What will need to be done before, during and after the event? What equipment will we need?

4. **Implementing plans**—How do we put our plans into effect?

a. Who will do what task?

b. Who will serve as the overall supervisor?

c. What is our timetable for getting different steps done?

5. **Evaluation**—Did the program do what it was intended to do?

a. *Methods.* What do we want programmers after us to know about this program? What methods can we use to get the information we need? When is the best time to conduct an evaluation?

b. *Content.* Did the program run smoothly? Was sufficient time allowed for planning and implementation? What should we do next time that we didn't do this time? Who came to the program? How did the people who came respond to the program? Did we achieve our goals and objectives? What need does the audience still have that we can plan a new program for?

Organizations Offering Professional Development Opportunities Suitable for FSA's

1. **Advanced Training Institute for International Student Advisers,** International Student Advisers Office, 717 East River Road, University of Minnesota, Minneapolis, Minnesota 55455

2. **Culture Learning Institute,** East-West Center, 1777 East-West Road, Honolulu, Hawaii 96848

3. **Developing Effective Skills for Working with International Students and Scholars,** Continuing Education Program, University of Delaware, Newark, Delaware 19711

4. **School for International Training,** Experiment in International Living, Brattleboro, Vermont 05301

5. **Society for Intercultural Education,** Training, and Research, 1414 Twenty-second Street, N.W., Washington, D.C. 20037

6. **Stanford Institute for Intercultural Communication,** P.O. Box A-B, Stanford, California 94305

Reference List

Althen, G. Intercultural communication central to educational exchange. *NAFSA Newsletter* 29(8), May-June 1978, 16-18.

Althen, G. (Ed.) *Students from the Arab world and Iran.* Washington, D.C.: National Association for Foreign Student Affairs, 1979.

Althen, G. (Ed.) *Learning across cultures.* Washington, D.C.: National Association for Foreign Student Affairs, 1981.

Althen, G. *Learning with your foreign roommate* (Rev. Ed.). Iowa City: University of Iowa, 1982.

Althen, G. & Riahinejad, A.R. Political depression among students from Iran. *NAFSA Newsletter* 33(6), April/May 1982, 129, 152-154.

Althen, G. & Stott, F. Counseling students with unrealistic academic objectives. *Personnel and Guidance Journal,* June, 1983.

Barnlund, D.C. *Public and private self in Japan and the United States.* Tokyo: The Simul Press, 1975.

Barr, M.J. & Keating, L.A. (Eds.). *Establishing effective programs.* (New Directions for Student Services, No. 7) San Francisco: Jossey-Bass, Inc., 1979.

Bates, J.D. *Writing with precision: How to write so you cannot possibly be misunderstood.* Washington, D.C.: Acropolis Books, Ltd., 1978.

Berlo, D.K. *The process of communication.* New York: Holt, Rinehart & Winston, 1960.

Bliss, E.C. *Getting things done.* New York: Bantam, 1978.

Boettinger, H.M. *Moving mountains, or the art and craft of letting others see things your way.* London: The Macmillan Company, 1969.

Brislin, R.W. *Cross-cultural encounters: Face-to-face interaction.* New York: Pergamon Press, 1981.

Church, A.T. Sojourner adjustment. *Psychological Bulletin* 91(3), 1982, 540-572.

Cole, M. & Scribner, S. *Culture and thought.* New York: John Wiley & Sons, 1974.

Condon, J.C. & Yousef, F. *An introduction to intercultural communication.* Indianapolis: Bobbs-Merrill, 1975.

Corsini, R. (Ed.). *Current psychotherapies.* Itasca, Ill.: F.E. Peacock Publishers, Inc., 1973.

Davey, W.G. (Ed.). *Intercultural theory and practice: A case method approach.* Washington, D.C.: Society for Intercultural Education, Training and Research, 1981.

Ellis, A. (Ed.) *Growth through reason: Verbatim cases in rational emotive therapy.* Palo Alto, Calif.: Science and Behavior, 1971.

Ellis, A. *Reason and emotion in psychotherapy.* New York: Lyle Stuart, 1972.

Ellis, A. *Humanistic psychotherapy: The rational-emotive approach.* New York: McGraw-Hill Book Company, 1973.

Ellis, A. *Executive leadership: A rational approach.* New York: Institute for Rational Living, 1978.

Ellis, A. & Harper, R.A. *A new guide to rational living.* No. Hollywood, Calif.: Wilshire Book Company, 1977.

Fanning, T. & Fanning, R. *Get it all done and still be human.* Radnor, Penn.: Chilton, 1979.

Feig, J.P. & Blair, J.G. *There is a difference: 17 intercultural perspectives.* Washington, D.C.: Meridian House, 1980.

Fisher, R. & Ury, W. *Getting to yes.* Boston: Houghton Mifflin, 1981.

Fordyce, J.K. & Weil, R. *Managing with people* (2nd Ed.). Reading, Mass.: Addison-Wesley Publishing Company, 1979.

Foust, S., *et al.* Dynamics of cross-cultural adjustment: From pre-arrival to re-entry. In G. Althen (Ed.), *Learning across cultures.* Washington, D.C.: National Association for Foreign Student Affairs, 1981.

Goodwin, C.D. & Nacht, M. *Absence of decision.* New York: Institute of International Education, 1983.

Gordon, T. *Leader effectiveness training.* New York: Wyden Books, 1977.

Gordon, T. *Parent effectiveness training.* New York: Peter H. Wyden, Inc., 1970.

Hall, E.T. *Beyond culture.* Garden City, N.Y.: Anchor Books, 1976.

Hanson, P.G. What to look for in groups. In J.W. Pfeiffer & J.E. Jones (Eds.), *Small-group training theory and practice.* La Jolla, Calif.: University Associates, n.d., 23-26.

Hanvey, R.G. *An attainable global perspective.* New York: Global Perspective in Education, n.d.

Hammer, M.R., Gudykunst, W.B., & Wiseman, R.L. Dimensions of intercultural effectiveness: An exploratory study. *International Journal of Intercultural Relations* 2(4), Winter 1978, 382-392.

Horner, D. & Vandersluis, K., *et al.* Cross-cultural counseling. In G. Althen (Ed.), *Learning across cultures.* Washington, D.C.: National Association for Foreign Student Affairs, 1981.

Ivey, A.E. & Authrer, J. *Microcounseling: Innovations in interviewing, counseling, psychotherapy, and psychoeducation.* Springfield, Illinois: C.C. Thomas, 1978.

Jones, J.E. A model of group development. In J.W. Pfeiffer & J.E. Jones (Eds.), *Small-group training theory and practice.* La Jolla: University Associates, n.d., 38-41.

Kluckhohn, C. & Kluckhohn, F. Values and value orientations in the theory of action: An exploration in definition and classification. In T. Parsons & E. Shils (Eds.), *Toward a general theory of action.* Cambridge: Harvard University Press, 1951.

Kohls, L.R. *Developing intercultural awareness.* Washington, D.C.: Society for Intercultural Education, Training, and Research, 1981.

Kohls, L.R. *Survival kit for overseas living.* Chicago: Intercultural Press, 1979.

Kuhn, T.S. *The structure of scientific revolutions.* (2nd ed., enlarged). Chicago: University of Chicago Press, 1970.

Lakein, A. *How to get control of your time and your life.* New York: The New American Library, 1973.

Lanham, R.A. *Revising prose.* New York: Charles Scribner's Sons, 1979.

Lebra, T.S. *Japanese patterns of behavior.* Honolulu: The University of Hawaii Press, 1976.

Lee, M.Y., Abd-Ella, M., & Burks, L.A. *Needs of foreign students from developing nations at U.S. colleges and universities.* Washington, D.C.: National Association for Foreign Student Affairs, 1981.

Mackenzie, R.A. *The time trap.* New York: AMACOM, 1972.

Mestenhauser, J.A. Are we professionals, semi-professionals, or dedicated good guys? *NAFSA Newsletter* 27(8), May 1976, 7, 9-11.

Mestenhauser, J.A. Do we have standards? *NAFSA Newsletter* 28(5), February 1977, 1, 3.

Mestenhauser, J.A. Foreign students as teachers: Lessons from the program in learning with foreign students. In G. Althen (Ed.), *Learning across cultures.* Washington, D.C.: National Association for Foreign Student Affairs, 1981.

Mestenhauser, J.A. Institutional strategies in the international exchange field. Paper presented at the Michigan State University International Year Conference, East Lansing, April 1982.

Nash, D. *Community in limbo.* Bloomington, Ind.: Indiana University Press, 1970.

National Association for Foreign Student Affairs. *Selection and admission of foreign students.* (Guideline Series 2). Washington, D.C., 1978.

National Association for Foreign Student Affairs. *Standards and responsi-bilities in international educational interchange* (Guideline Series 1). Washington, D.C. 1979.

National Association for Foreign Student Affairs. *Foreign alumni: Over-seas links for U.S. institutions.* Washington, D.C., 1980.

National Association for Foreign Student Affairs. *Orientation of foreign students.* (Guideline Series 4). Washington, D.C., 1980.

National Association for Foreign Student Affairs. *Adviser's manual of fed-eral regulations affecting foreign students and scholars.* Washing-ton, D.C., 1982 (partially revised in 1983).

Parker, O.D. *Cultural clues to the Middle Eastern student.* Washington, D.C.: American Friends of the Middle East (now called AMIDEAST), 1977.

Pedersen, P.P. *et al.* (Eds.). *Counseling across cultures* (Rev. and expanded ed.). Honolulu: The University of Hawaii Press, 1981.

Peter, L. & Hull, R. *The Peter principle.* New York: Bantam Press, 1970.

Peterson, D. Seductivity of stereotypes. *NAFSA Newsletter* 29(4), January 1978, 5-6.

Pusch, M.D. (Ed.). *Multicultural education: A cross-cultural training approach.* Chicago: Intercultural Press, Inc., 1979.

Pusch, M.D. *et al.* Cross-cultural training. In G. Althen (Ed.), *Learning across cultures.* Washington, D.C.: National Association for Foreign Student Affairs, 1981.

Renwick, G.W. Toward an understanding of our professional ethics. *NAFSA Newsletter* 28(5), February 1977, 1-3, 5, 14-15.

Renwick, G.W. *Evaluation handbook for cross-cultural training and mul-ticultural education.* Chicago: Intercultural Press, Inc., 1981.

Rhinesmith, S.H. *Bring home the world.* New York: AMACOM, 1975.

Rogers, C.R. *Client-centered therapy.* Boston: Houghton Mifflin Company, 1965.

Samovar, L.A., Porter, R.E., & Jain, N.C. *Understanding intercultural communication.* Belmont, Calif.: Wadsworth Publishing Company, 1981.

Schindler-Rainman, E. & Lippitt, R. *Taking your meetings out of the doldrums.* San Diego: University Associates, 1975.

Scott, D. *How to put more time in your life.* New York: The New Ameri-can Library, Inc., 1980.

Spaulding, S. & Flack, M.J. *The world's students in the United States.* New York: Praeger, 1976.

Stewart, E.C. *American cultural patterns: A cross-cultural perspective.* Chicago: Intercultural Press, Inc., 1972.

Story, K.E. The student development professional and the foreign student: A conflict of values? *Journal of College Student Personnel*, January 1982, 66-70.

Townsend, R. *Up the organization*. New York: Fawcett Crest, 1970.

Walen, S.R., DiGiuseppe, R. & Wessler, R.l. *A practitioner's guide to rational-emotive therapy*. New York: Oxford University Press, 1980.

Walsh, J.E. *Humanistic culture learning*. Honolulu: The University of Hawaii Press, 1979.

Zinsser, W. *On writing well* (2nd Ed.). New York: Harper & Row, Publishers, 1980.

Index

AACRAO. *See* American Association of Collegiate Registrars and Admissions Officers

African-American Institute (AAI): address of, 158; relations with, 51, 115-16

Abd-Ella, M., 58, 128

Absence of Decision, 7n

Active listening, 91

Administration of a foreign student office, 75-86, 125-26

Admission of foreign students, 96-98, 160-63

Advanced Training Institute for International Student Advisers, 195

Advice, 102-3; immigration, 6-7

Adviser's Manual of Federal Regulations Affecting Foreign Students and Scholars, 66-67, 69

Advising and counseling foreign students, guidelines on, 101-8; principles for, 166-68; skills in, 88-95

Agency for International Development (AID) and the National Association for Foreign Student Affairs, 35

ALIGU. *See* American Language Institute of George Washington University

Althen, G., 64

Alumni, foreign, 121-22

Ambiguity, tolerance for, 24-25

American (the term), 1n

American Association of Collegiate Registrars and Admissions Officers (AACRAO): address of, 158; publications of, 56

American Council for Nationalities Service, 158

American Cultural Patterns, 64

American culture, 26

American Language Institute of George Washington University, (ALIGU), 60

America-Mideast Educational and Training Services (AMIDEAST), address of, 158; relations with, 51

Applied linguistics, 59-60

Assumptions and values, cultural differences in, 62

Attorney, retaining an immigration, 70

Attribution error, 47

Authrer, J. 95

Awareness, 92-93, 107. *See also* Self-awareness

Barnlund, D., 63, 149, 176

Barr, M., 119

Bates, J., 73

Berlo, D., 72

Blair, J., 56

Bliss, E., 81

Boettinger, H., 74

Bostain, J., 21

Bring Home the World, 121